# ADVANCED PHOTOSHOP CS2 TRICKERY & FX

# ADVANCED PHOTOSHOP CS2 TRICKERY & FX

## STEPHEN BURNS

CHARLES RIVER MEDIA, INC.

Hingham, Massachusetts

Cover Design: The Printed Image
Cover Images: Stephen Burns

CHARLES RIVER MEDIA, INC.
10 Downer Avenue
Hingham, Massachusetts 02043
781-740-0400
781-740-8816 (FAX)
info@charlesriver.com
www.charlesriver.com

This book is printed on acid-free paper.

Stephen Burns. *Advanced Photoshop CS2 Trickery & FX.*
ISBN: 1-58450-447-1

Library of Congress Cataloging-in-Publication Data
Burns, Stephen, 1963-
    Advanced Photoshop CS2 trickery & FX / Stephen Burns.— 1st ed.
        p. cm.
    Includes index.
    ISBN 1-58450-447-1 (alk. paper)
    1.   Computer graphics. 2.   Adobe Photoshop.
 I. Title: Advanced Photoshop CS2 trickery and FX. II.
Title: Photoshop CS2 trickery. III. Title.
    T385.B86434 2006
    006.6'86—dc22
                                    2005025990

Printed in the United States of America
05 7 6 5 4 3 2 First Edition

This book is dedicated to my mom and dad
for having inspired me to always excel at what I do.
They are excellent parents.

# CONTENTS

# ACKNOWLEDGMENTS

Without the support of so many others this book would not have been possible.

I would like to thank Jenifer Niles, Meg Dunkerley, Lance Morganelli, Bryan Davidson, and Phil Timper for their patience and professionalism in seeing this book to fruition properly.

Thanks to Janis Wendt and Josh Haftel, and the rest of the Nik Multimedia team for their ever-growing encouragement and support. Great job guys on producing a super plug-in package for Photoshop.

Finally, I feel it is only appropriate to thank Adobe and Newtek for creating such outstanding software. And I would like to thank the members of the San Diego Photoshop Users group (*www.sdphotoshopusers.com*) for their dedication and support in helping me build a strong network of digital artists from which I continually draw inspiration.

# FOREWORD

What is Art? What makes someone an Artist? Is a computer a valid art tool? Is a computer an *incredible* art tool? What's your favorite color?

Tough questions? For some. For Stephen Burns, one of the hardest working, Artists, Instructors, Inspirers I have the pleasure of knowing, they are moot (all except the "What's your favorite color?" one, he's pretty un-committed on that issue).

For me, Art is about passion, and about communicating that passion through created imagery and objects, words, sounds, and movement. Stephen Burns is extremely passionate about Art, and about communicating that passion through the works that he creates (and shares with the world in his numerous gallery exhibitions). But even more importantly (especially for those of you holding this book), he is passionate about communicating his thoughts and technical processes *behind* what he creates. And that is where this book comes in.

In these pages you'll follow Stephen along on many different artistic journeys–each one geared to giving you the advanced Photoshop CS2 "trickery" needed to create your own visions, often out of thin air. This intensive nuts-and-bolts instruction into our beloved Photoshop is combined with Stephen's artistic insights into light and color, composition and eye flow, and (among other things) the need for maintaining synchronistic spontaneity as part of the creative process, especially within the often left-brained art studio of the computer.

Bottom line, get ready for an E-ticket creative roller coaster ride with the unstoppable Stephen Burns–one that is sure to inspire you in your own passionate endeavors!

Jack Davis
Author, Photographer, "Artist"
*www.HowToWowTraining.com*

# PREFACE

This is a very exciting time for artists because they are faced with a medium that represents the 20th and 21st century. The medium that I refer to is the computer. The computer has been around for several decads now, and today's software for artists is not only in great abundance but much easier to use, so artists are learning how to express themselves effectively with it.

In my first book *Photoshop CS Trickery & FX* we took a journey to learn the digital medium so that we could spend more time using our artistic voices and less time struggling with the technical learning curve that digital tools often present. Learning digital tools is essentially like learning another language or artistic skill like music, writing, filmmaking. They all take time and lots of practice. The advantage that you have as a digital artist, however, is that your medium, the computer, combines all creative art forms. What does this mean to you as an artist? Well, it's simple. You can create by combining any or all of the art forms to communicate on a whole new level.

In this book, we will continue the creative journey with exposure to the traditional approach to creating, so that you can make a stronger connection to how things were done in the past. Having an insight into the past will not only help you with understanding the terminology being used in Photoshop CS2, but will also give you insight to what is happening during the creative process and why. As time and technology progress traditional concepts are taught and used less frequently by a lot of artists. So for those of you who started creating digitally, this background information should help spawn some new creativity.

This book will give you an insight as to how and why Photoshop CS2 functions as it does. Much of this is discussed in chapters 1 and 2. The rest of the book will share with you in-depth steps as to how the projects in the book were created. I have also covered a little bit of 3D creation, not for the purpose of instructing you in 3D applications but to share the possibilities that this medium can provide for you. I have included some LightWave 3D screen shots to give you a peak into the program, so use the finished images provided and have fun with the exercises.

I wrote this book in the spirit of sharing my insights about the creative approaches to manipulating your digital photographs into your own masterpieces. My hope is that it will serve to bring together both the traditional and technical approaches to creativity, so that you will gain a better understanding of how they can work together and be able to apply that knowledge to your own creations.

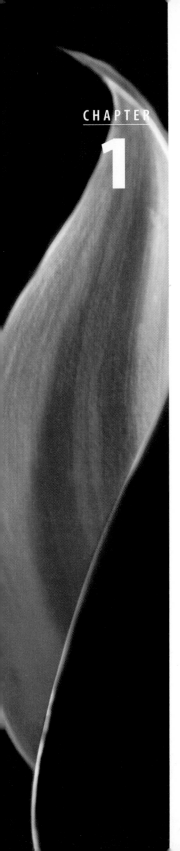

# CHAPTER

# 1

# SIMPLIFYING THE INTERFACE

In my first book, *Photoshop CS Trickery & FX*, we took a journey to understand our digital medium so that we can spend more time developing our artistic voices and less time struggling with the challenging technical learning curve. We are learning another language and unfortunately this takes time. However, the more we use it the more we will become fluent with its dialect. This is no different from learning any other creative medium, such as music, writing, filmmaking, painting, drawing, or sculpture. The advantage that you have as a digital artist is the fact that your medium—the computer—combines all creative art forms. What does this mean to you as an artist? It's simple. You can create by combining any or all of the art forms to communicate on a whole new level.

Throughout this journey you will be exposed to the traditional or analog approach to creating so that you can start to make a connection about how things were done in the past. Having an insight into the past not only helps us with understanding the terminology being used in Photoshop CS2, but also serves as insight about what we are doing throughout the creative process. However, as time and technology progresses, traditional concepts are slipping further away from today's students. Their exposure from the beginning is not based on analog technology; instead, it is based on digital. It will be interesting to see what type of artists this new age will produce.

The intention of this chapter is not to provide an intensive listing of all of the tools and commands in Photoshop CS2. We will assume that you already have a basic un-

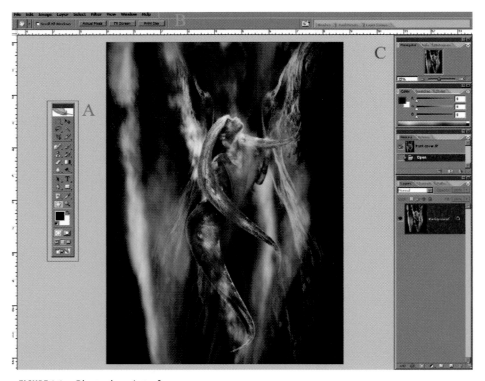

**FIGURE 1.1**   Photoshop interface.

derstanding of the Photoshop CS2 interface. However, we will cover some of the new features in CS2 briefly here and extensively in the following tutorials.

As you work through the tutorials be patient and enjoy the process. The digital industry tells us that within a few clicks we can create masterpieces. However, it's a little more challenging than that because not only must we have an understanding of composition and our traditional expertise like photography or painting, but also we must learn the new digital language so that we can create intuitively. It is not expected that you will create images such as the ones in this book overnight. However, you will benefit from the author's experience and insight in digital artistry. So let's begin and have fun together.

There are only three places that you will access the commands in Photoshop CS2. They are tools bar, menus, and palettes (see Figure 1.1).

## TOOLS BAR

The tools bar is the vertical slender bar that houses a visual representation of the variety of brushes and tools that you will use in your creations (see Figure 1.2). When each one is clicked, the options bar changes accordingly, because like a painter, we usually don't want to apply 100% of our pigment to the canvas. Normally we will start in lower opacities to build form, saturation, and density over time.

The first section is the selection tools. All of these tools will tell the program to effect only those pixels inside the animated dotted line (marching ants) created with a selection tool (see Figure 1.3). Notice that the small black triangle on the bottom right corner of the tools icon indicates that there are more options available, as shown in Figure 1.4. Click and hold that tool to reveal the other options. Those options will appear in a drop-down menu.

**FIGURE 1.3**
Selection tools.

**FIGURE 1.4**    Other options in the Tools icons.

**FIGURE 1.2**
Tools bar.

The next section lists all of the painting tools for applying painting and photographic effects (see Figure 1.5). Figure 1.6 shows the vector graphic tools for creating resolution-less imagery. This set primarily utilizes the Pen tool, as well as text, drawing vector shapes, and editing paths.

Finally, we have the annotation tool set for embedding notes to your printer or client in the file. This set of tools allows you to sample color, zoom in and out, and navigate around your document after zooming (see Figure 1.7). As we work we will use the Painting and the Selection tools quite regularly.

**FIGURE 1.6**
Vector tools.

**FIGURE 1.7**
Annotation tools.

**FIGURE 1.5**
Painting tools on the Tools bar.

## MENUS

The second place that you will access Photoshop's commands are the drop-down menus. The term *menu* refers to cascading text menus along the top left side of the interface, as shown in Figure 1.8. Within each one of these are submenus that provide access to deeper commands within the program.

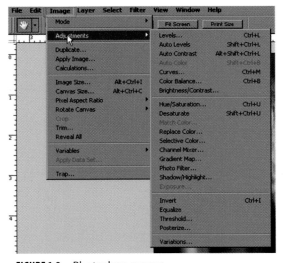

**FIGURE 1.8**    Photoshop menus.

## PALETTES

The third and last place that you will access Photoshop's commands are the palettes. Palettes are visual shortcuts to many of the commands that can be found in the text menus. For those who do not have a dual monitor setup, palettes can be "docked" or located on the menu bar on the top right corner of the interface for space-saving organization. Just click and hold on the tab of the palette and drag it into the docking bar. Notice that all palettes have a drop-down menu that looks like a small black triangle located on the top right corner, as shown in Figure 1.9. This gives you other options for that palette. There are two highlighted submenus, which are new to CS2 called New Layer Group from Layers and Group into New Smart Object. You will be using these extensively throughout the tutorials.

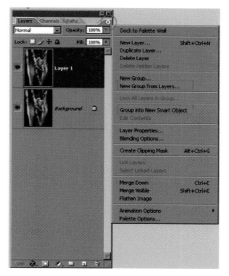

**FIGURE 1.9**    Photoshop palettes.

## UNDERSTANDING THE PAINTBRUSH ENGINE

Since Photoshop 6.0, the Paintbrush engine has gone through extensive changes. You can now produce effects like fire, smoke, sparks, and textures by using the Paintbrush animated options. This engine has been optimized to use a digitized pen like that of the WACOM tablet. For more information about this product go to *www.wacom.com*. Let's get to know the basics of animating, altering brush properties, and saving custom brushes.

When you click on the Paintbrush icon shown in Figure 1.10, notice the options bar. Click on the Brush Preset Picker as shown in Figure 1.11.

**FIGURE 1.11**    Options bar for the Paint tool.

**FIGURE 1.10**
Photoshop
Paint tool.

A drop-down menu of default paint strokes is listed. You can resize this menu by clicking on the bottom right corner of the palette and pulling it to any size to see more options. If you click the Oak Leaf brush as shown in Figure 1.12, you can view its variable brush properties in the Brush palette (Windows > Brushes).

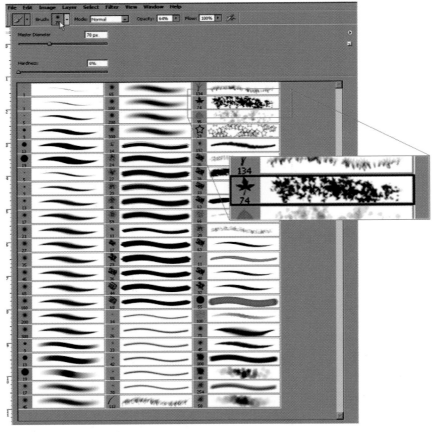

**FIGURE 1.12**    Animated properties of the Oak Leaf brush.

## CREATING YOUR OWN ANIMATED PAINTBRUSH

Now let's see how each dynamic works to create a single animated brush. Figures 1.13 to 1.15 illustrate this process.

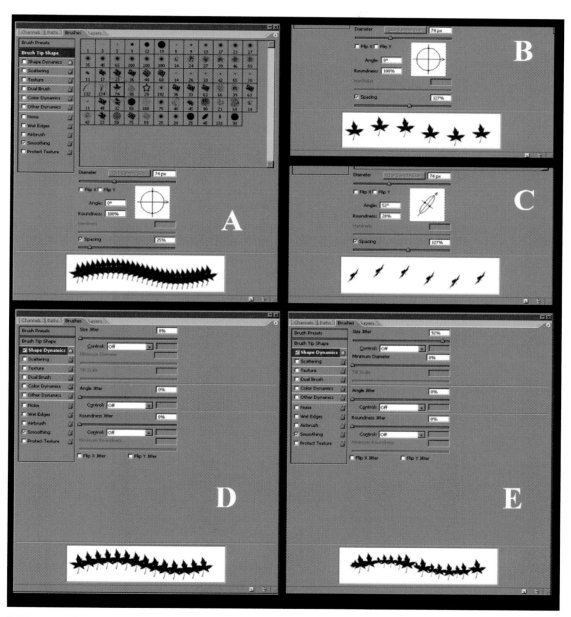

**FIGURE 1.13**    Illustrations A–E.

### Step 1

Select the Oak Leaf brush and clear the checkbox of all its animated properties. Figure 1.13A illustrates what you should see. At the bottom of the Brush palette, play with the spacing scroll bar and notice that the preview window updates automatically (see Figure 1.13B).

Additionally, play with the diameter by clicking the dots on the outside of the circle and altering the shape and rotation of the brush (see Figure 1.13C).

### Step 2

Click on the Shape Dynamics layer to get the option for it, which is listed on the right. The stroke of the brush in the preview window should show one continuous size and spacing (see Figure 1.13D).

### Step 3

Adjust your jitter to 92% and notice the stroke update in the preview window, as shown in Figure 1.13E. Jitter is simply the random application of a technique over the length of the stroke. The higher the percentage the more drastic and varied the technique.

### Step 4

Play with the minimum diameter slider and watch how the size of the stroke is varied over time (see Figure 1.14F).

### Step 5

As you adjust the angle jitter slider, notice that the brush applies a percentage of rotation over the length of each stroke. This is great for debris and cloud effects (see Figure 1.14G).

### Step 6

As you play with the roundness jitter notice that this option allows you to apply the full diameter of your mouse shape or squish it for an elliptical effect over the length of the stroke (see Figure 1.14H).

### Step 7

Play with the minimum roundness jitter to set the minimum distortion that you want to apply to your image. In conjunction with the other properties, this adds a little more control (see Figure 1.14I).

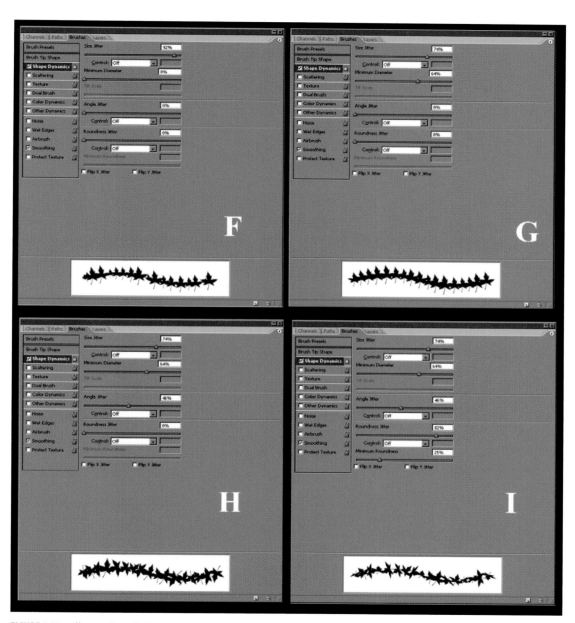

**FIGURE 1.14**    Illustrations F–I.

### Step 8

Click on the scattering layer and watch what happens in your preview window, as shown in Figure 1.15J. This is a favorite brush property—it's great for explosions.

### Step 9

Slide the count slider to the right to add more of the brush effect to the scatter. The two in combination can be visually powerful (see Figure 1.15K).

### Step 10

Click on the texture to add presets to your brush pattern, as shown in Figure 1.15L.

### Step 11

When you click on the Dual Brush options, as shown in Figure 1.15M, Photoshop allows you to add custom brush presets to your current animated brush.

### Step 12

Change the colors of your foreground and background swatches by clicking on the (front or foreground) color swatch near the bottom of the tools palette to bring up the color picker. You can choose a color for that swatch and play with each of the sliders to understand their effects. There is no preview for this in the stroke window so you will have to play with each property by drawing on a layer filled with white.

### Step 13

Select the Other Dynamics layer. Here you can tell the brush engine how to apply the effects. Your options can be set to apply the technique with the WACOM Pen's pressure sensitivity, fade over a specified number of pixels, and use the pen tilt, stylus wheel, or pen rotation. The WACOM tablet is a wonderful tool for artists with a painting background. One of its great attributes is its ability to apply the density of a color or an effect based on the pressure applied to the tablet's pen. The Intuos 2 and 3 have up to 1024 levels of pressure sensitivity, which is double that of the Graphire, which has 512 levels of pressure. If you are on a budget the Graphire is the tool for you. However, if you want precise control and subtlety in the application of your technique, the Intuos line is a wonderful tool. Everyone has a preference in terms of the size of custom brushes, so keep in mind that any of your variable brush settings can be applied with the pen's pressure sensitivity.

After you have created your new animated brush you need to save it. Click on the small black triangle in the top right corner of the Brush palette. Select Save Brush Preset and name it appropriately.

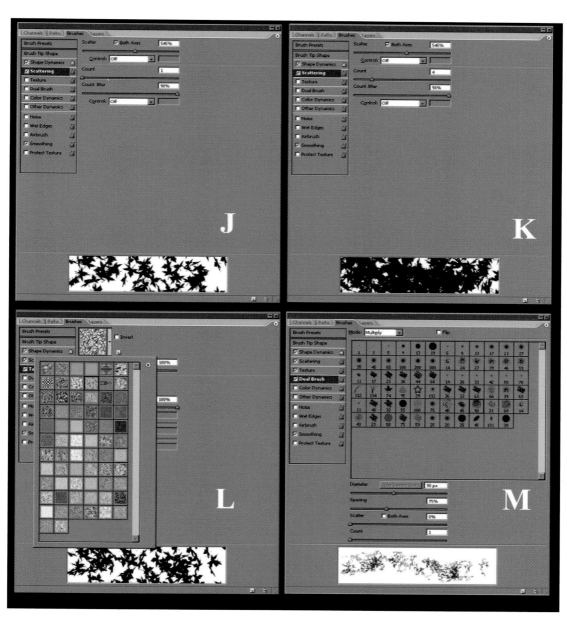

**FIGURE 1.15A**    Illustrations J–M.

## CREATING YOUR OWN CUSTOM BRUSH PALETTE

After you create a few custom brushes, you will want to create a custom brush palette. In Figure 1.16, the objective is to save the custom brushes that are highlighted in red into their own palette and discard the rest.

### Step 1

With your brush presets cascaded, click on the submenu icon and click on Preset Manager, as shown in Figure 1.17.

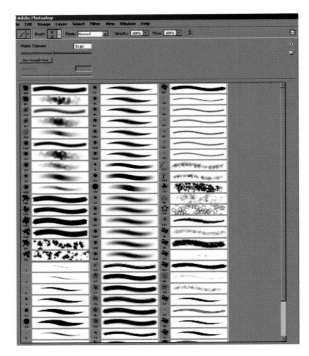

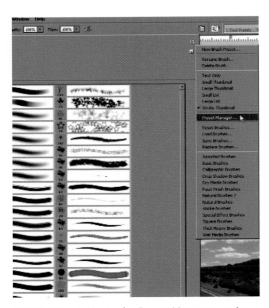

FIGURE 1.17    Activate the Preset Manager option.

FIGURE 1.16    Stroke Palette option.

### Step 2

Highlight all of the brushes that you are not interested in saving with a shift/click on the first and last brush. Now click Delete to discard them (see Figure 1.18).

Your Brush palette should now look something like Figures 1.19 and 1.20 in the stroke view on your Options palette.

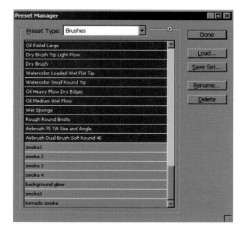

**FIGURE 1.18**    Highlight the brushes to delete them.

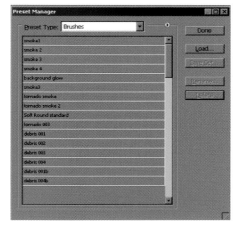

**FIGURE 1.19**    Final brushes in Preset Manager option.

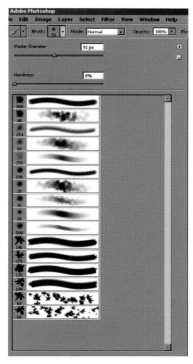

**FIGURE 1.20**    Brush stroke preview on the options bar.

## Step 3

Once you have your brushes, you must save them to access them at any time when you are creating. Therefore, access your Brush palette submenu and click Save Brushes. Next, navigate and create a folder that you know you will be able to find when you need access to your brushes. In this example, we call the folder on the desktop Custom Brushes (see Figures 1.21 and 1.22).

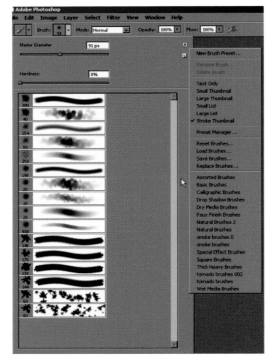

**FIGURE 1.21**  Saving brushes.

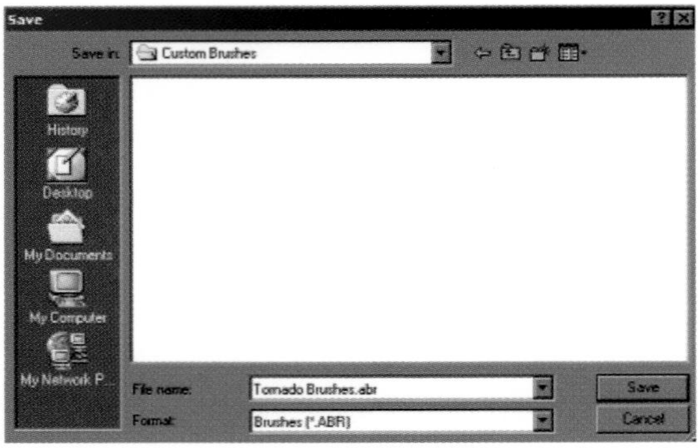

**FIGURE 1.22**  Saving brushes location.

Experiment with your brush settings and discover the wide range of creative uses of the brush engine. Also, be organized and save the brushes under meaningful names that relate to your workflow, for example, hairbrushes, smoke brushes, texture brushes, and so on. Now that you have an understanding of the brushes, let's take a look at the new Adobe Bridge interface.

## OVERVIEW OF ADOBE BRIDGE INTERFACE

If you wanted to preview your images in Photoshop CS you had to access the browser, which of course, was integrated with the CS interface. Now the browser functions as its own entity and has a separate icon for accessing it on your desktop or in your programs menu. The new browser is called Bridge, undoubtedly named as a bridge to all of the programs on your computer. In other words, Bridge will not only open graphic files in Photoshop, but also it will recognize any file on your system and open it in the appropriate program. As an example, it will recognize a Word document and open it in Microsoft Word or an InDesign document and open it in In-Design. In addition, Bridge will view and play movie formats.

The interface, as shown in Figure 1.23, looks very much like its predecessor.

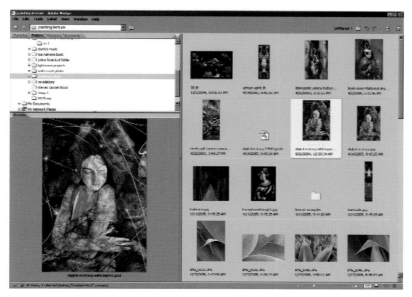

**FIGURE 1.23**    Adobe Bridge interface.

As shown in Figures 1.24 and 1.25, you can adjust the slider to resize your thumbnails on the lower right corner.

**FIGURE 1.24**    Reducing thumbnail size.

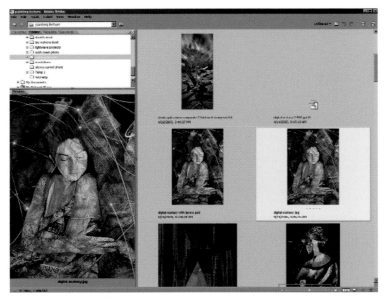

**FIGURE 1.25**   Increasing thumbnail size.

You have several viewing options, including the Filmstrip view. This allows you to see a larger version of your image while the rest are tiled horizontally along the bottom (see Figure 1.26).

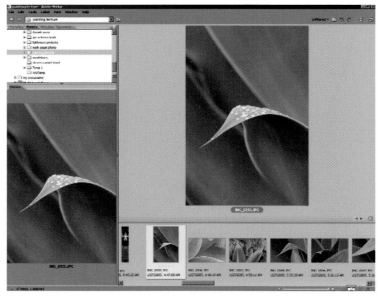

**FIGURE 1.26**   Filmstrip option in Bridge.

Next, you have the Details view, as shown in Figure 1.27 in case you need to see more information about a file.

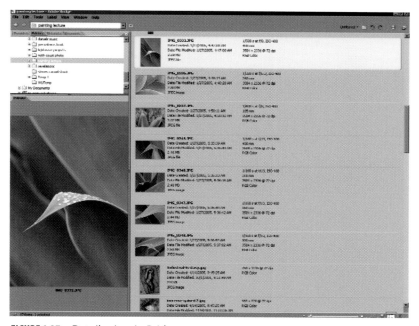

**FIGURE 1.27**    Details view in Bridge.

If you have a client who is previewing images that you have created, then the labeling method is handy for categorizing and giving rank to each of the files. Right-click the highlighted images and select the Label submenu to assign a color to the images (see Figure 1.28).

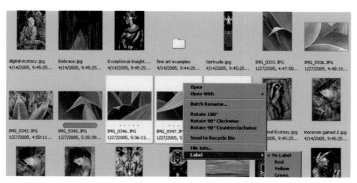

**FIGURE 1.28**    Designating color to thumbnails.

Once a color is designated to the thumbnails, you can click on the stars to designate a rank (see Figures 1.29 and 1.30).

Finally, you can assign a batch process by Ctrl-clicking several thumbnails, accessing Tools > Photoshop, and selecting your batch actions for the selected images. Notice the new Merge to HDR menu, as shown in Figure 1.31. It will be discussed in Chapter 3.

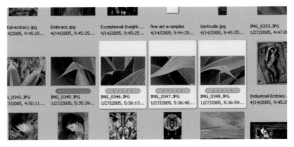

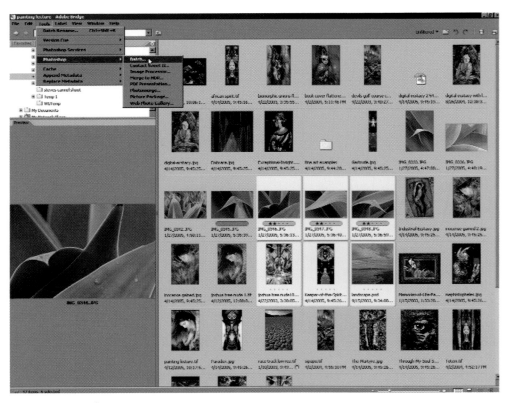

**FIGURE 1.30**    Altering the rank of thumbnails.

**FIGURE 1.29**    Ranked thumbnails.

**FIGURE 1.31**    Batch process menu.

## WORKFLOW IN BRIDGE

Bridge is optimized for a more effective workflow in terms of organizing your photos from the digital camera to your storage drive. In Bridge you can categorize your photos just by adding subfolders to a location on your hard drive. Knowing where all of your photos are located creates an effective organizational system. It is a good idea to have a separate hard drive to store all of your images. There are a number of external storage options on the market, so consider the number of photos that you capture regularly and purchase an external hard drive system for your needs. A lesser cost alternative is to purchase an external hard drive case for under $50.00. Then you can purchase any size hard drive that you need and place it into the case. Most of these external cases use USB or Firewire connections and come with a built-in fan to cool the storage device.

The external drive will register as a separate drive letter on your computer and it may be designated as a "Removable Disk" drive. Depending on the number of devices on your system it will be given a drive letter that will range from D to Z. Now, in Bridge, navigate to your external drive.

Make sure the Folder tab is selected in the top left window. The window where you would normally see your thumbnails will be blank, so right-click on this space and choose New Folder. Give the folder a name that best represents the photos that will be placed into it. For example, "Wedding Photos" or "Night Shots," or you can organize your shots by date. Within these folders you can add subfolders, such as "Night Shots in New York" and so on.

After you set up a variety of folders on your hard drive, navigate to any storage card that your camera used to deposit your files. You will usually see a folder called DCIM that will have subfolders with your digital photos stored in them. View your photos in Bridge on the right and make sure that can see your newly titled subfolders listed on the left. Drag and drop your images into the proper categories.

## CREATING KEYWORDS FOR EACH IMAGE

Now that you have organized all of your photos, you need to assign them key words so that if you need a particular image or a series of images you can plug in a search word such as "people" and all of the appropriate photos will be listed in the thumbnail view. The following steps explain the procedure.

### Step 1

Choose the Keywords tab above the preview window. By default you are given some predefined categories At this stage you will want to create your own categories, so right-click in the empty space of the keyword window and click New Keyword Set, as shown in Figure 1.32.

## Step 2

It is a good idea to make sure the title of the keyword set reflects the main category of the parent folder that each of the subfolders is located in. In this example it is titled Texture. Right-click on the Texture keyword set and select New Keyword. Make as many keywords that will define the images associated with Texture, as shown in Figure 1.33.

**FIGURE 1.32**   Create a new keyword set.

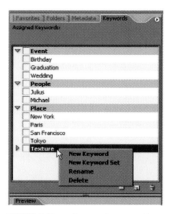

**FIGURE 1.33**   Create keywords to define images.

## Step 3

Next, highlight a series of images with a shift-click between the first and the final image or Ctrl-click on individual thumbnails. In the keyword panel, click on the checkbox to associate the proper keywords with the image or images. Note that if you select the Texture keyword set, all of the keywords in this category will be applied to your chosen thumbnails (see Figure 1.34).

## Step 4

Now let's test our search engine. Hit Ctrl-F to bring up the Find panel. In the Source section you can navigate to the folder or the subfolders that you would like to search in (see Figure 1.35).

## Step 5

Under the Criteria section select how you would like Find to search for your images. For this option choose keywords (see Figure 1.36).

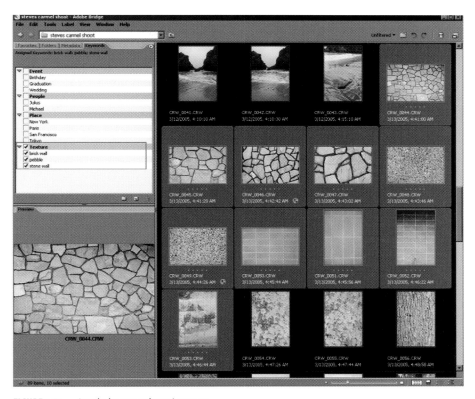

**FIGURE 1.34**    Apply keywords to images.

**FIGURE 1.35**    Find dialog panel.

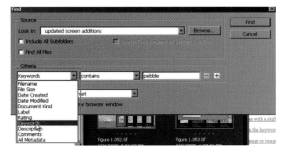

**FIGURE 1.36**    Choose keywords under criteria.

## Step 6

Next, define the parameters that the search engine will use to identify the images. In this case choose contains. Finally, enter the keyword that you would like to use. Pebble is used here (see Figure 1.37).

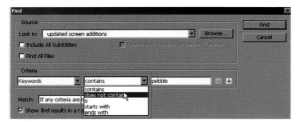

**FIGURE 1.37**    Criteria panel.

That's all there is to it. If you take a look at the thumbnails you will now see the particular images that were associated with the "pebble" search (see Figure 1.38).

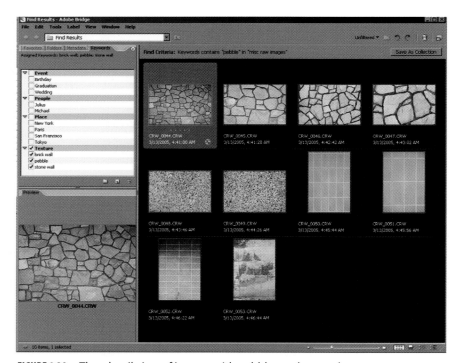

**FIGURE 1.38**    Thumbnail view of images with pebble as a keyword.

## THE RAW INTERFACE

Figure 1.39 shows an overview of the RAW interface. It shows the basic preview pane that takes up the bulk of the interface. The tonal, color, and effects controls are on the right and the workflow and resizing options are on the lower left. Note the histogram in the top right corner, which displays the tonal information representing the Red,

Green and Blue channels independently. Any information from the center to the left of the graph represents the middle to lower tonalities until it reaches black. Inversely, the center of the graph all the way to the right represents the middle to brighter tonalities toward white. A higher vertical mound indicates a greater amount of those particular tones and colors in your image. Let's move on.

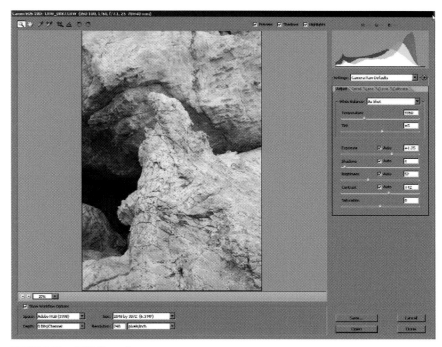

**FIGURE 1.39**    RAW interface.

ON THE CD

You may use your own RAW files; however, one has been provided on the CD-ROM in Tutorials/ch 1 original images/crw_0087.crw.

### Step 1

Click on each of the drop-down menus in the workflow area to preview your options for color space, bit depth, sizing, and resolution, as shown in Figures 1.40 through 1.42.

**FIGURE 1.40**    RAW interface color space options.

**FIGURE 1.41**    RAW interface color depth options.

**FIGURE 1.42**    RAW interface sizing and resolution.

## Step 2

Take a look at the color temperature slider under the Adjust tab and slide it to the right and left. Notice that as you slide to the right your image becomes warmer (yellow) and as you drag in the opposite direction your image becomes cooler (blue). The histogram in the top right gives you an update as to how all of the colors are responding to any and all adjustments in the RAW interface (see Figures 1.43 and 1.44).

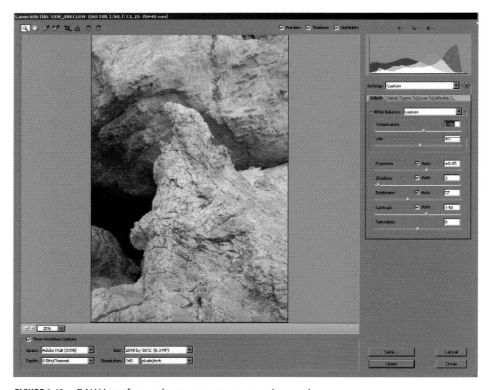

**FIGURE 1.43**    RAW interface color temperature warming options.

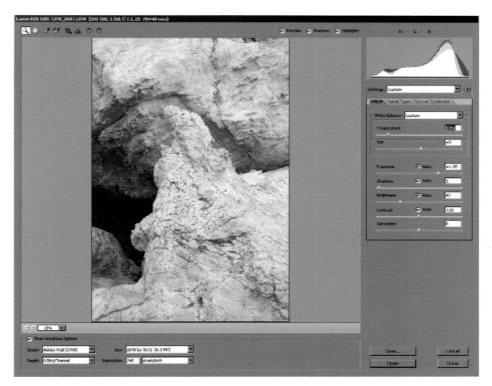

**FIGURE 1.44**    RAW interface color temperature cooling options.

### Step 3

Experiment with the Tint slider and see how you can control magenta and green. This is great for situations where textures are photographed near fluorescent lighting situations. Note how your histogram displays a dominant magenta or yellow, moving higher as you adjust the Tint slider to the right or left (see Figures 1.45 and 1.46).

### Step 4

Take a look at the exposure slider and notice that it will help you make adjustment to any over- or underexposed images. Click the Preview and Shadows tab in the top right and adjust the slider so that your image becomes darker (Figure 1.47). Look closely at the shadow region. If a blue colored tint previews in these areas then your shadows will have no detail. Since detail is an important matter for texturing we should use the preview option regularly.

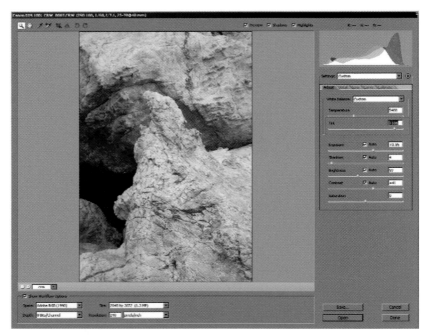

**FIGURE 1.45**    RAW interface color tinting toward magenta.

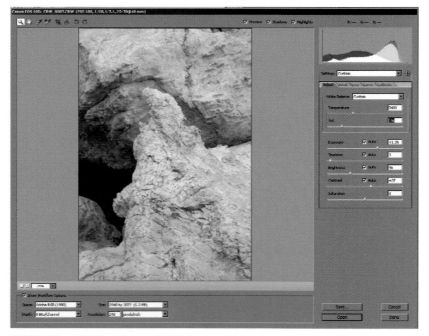

**FIGURE 1.46**    RAW interface color tinting toward green.

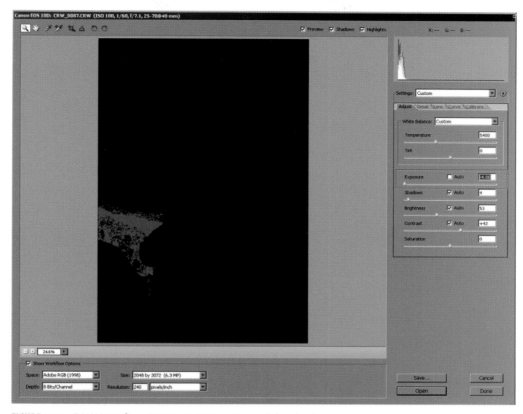

**FIGURE 1.47**    RAW Interface Exposure Option toward the shadows.

## Step 5

Now, do the same thing and adjust your image so that it goes almost white (Figure 1.48). Make sure the Preview and Highlights boxes are checked. Any area that is red will have no detail.

Figure 1.49 shows the image that is properly adjusted with details in both shadows and highlights.

Since you are dealing with the raw file data you have more information to play with than if it were formatted. In other words, you have at your command the raw ones and zeroes that the camera originally captured. Once your adjustments are applied and you save the file, it is formatted as a Tiff, Jpeg, or PSD of your choice.

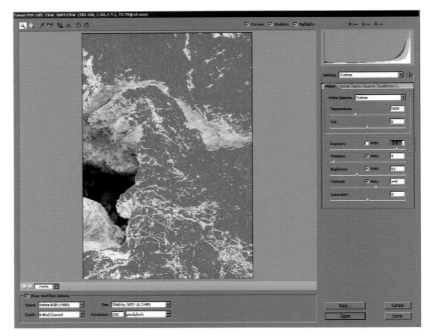

**FIGURE 1.48**    RAW Interface Exposure Option toward the highlights.

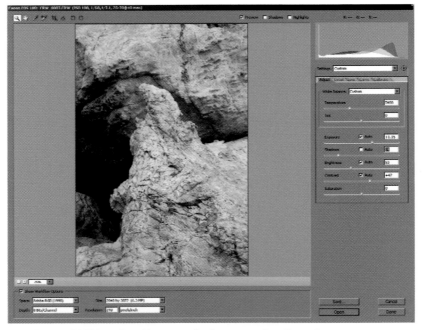

**FIGURE 1.49**    RAW Interface Exposure Option properly adjusted.

## WHAT YOU HAVE LEARNED

- A brief overview of the organization of the interface
- The three sections of the interface to access all commands
- A brief explanation of the tools palette
- A brief explanation of cascading menus
- How to create and save animated brushes; how to save the entire brush palette
- Command palettes as shortcuts to what you can access in the cascading menus
- Adobe Bridge and some of the new features in Photoshop CS2
- The RAW interface

Now let's move on to a deeper understanding of how Photoshop CS2 works.

# MASTERING PHOTOSHOP FUNDAMENTALS

**IN THIS CHAPTER**

- How and why layer blend modes work
- How an 8-bit environment functions
- The importance of selections and how to create them
- How to save selections
- The connection between masks and channels
- How to create and edit alpha channels
- The application of layer masks

## Layer Blend Modes

Use the blend modes to take advantage of ways to blend layers to produce dynamic and creative results.

There is a drop-down menu at the top left-hand corner of our layer palette where our layer blend modes reside. By default it reads Normal. We will take a close look at three of the blend mode sections and discover what they can do and how they do it.

To view the blend modes you must make sure that you have a layer highlighted and not the background. The background is your base canvass. It is not a layer, so as a matter of procedure, duplicate your background (Ctrl-J) so that Photoshop creates the image on its own layer. Now you will have access to your blend modes.

Notice in Figure 2.1, that there are three large sections separated by a thick black line. The first section blends the highlighted layer with the layer underneath so that all of the blacks are maintained and the whites go completely transparent.

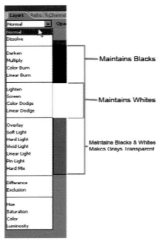

**FIGURE 2.1**    Blending the different layers.

The second section blends the highlighted layer with the layer underneath so that all of the whites are maintained and the blacks go completely transparent.

The third section blends the highlighted layer with the layer underneath so that all of the blacks and whites are maintained and the medium grays (midtones) go completely transparent. Let's prove this theory.

*Throughout the rest of this chapter we will work through a variety of exercises that outline important Photoshop fundamentals.*

The next exercise shows two images that illustrate how the blend mode works. The first is an example of how the gradient is affected and the second shows how the duplicate layer responds with itself.

## Step 1

ON THE CD

Open the cactus.jpg from the CD-ROM Tutorials/ch 2 original images folder in Photoshop and create a new layer. Press the D key to set the foreground and background color to black and white.

## Step 2

Select your gradient tool. Starting from left to right, click and drag on your canvass while holding down the Shift key. The Shift key will constrain the flow to one direction. You have just created a fill made up of 256 shades of gray. The blend mode is at normal so the integrity of the gradient is maintained (see Figure 2.2).

**FIGURE 2.2**    Effects of the Normal blend mode on a duplicate layer.

Now let's see the effects of each gradient as we apply our blend modes.

*In the next steps you will see two examples. One will show the effects of the blend mode applied to the gradient and the other will show the results of the blend mode applied to a duplicate layer. This will give you both an understanding of how tonal information is altered as well as a practical view of how photographic images are affected.*

## Section 1

**Darken:** Whites go transparent; however, some residual of midtone still persists (see Figure 2.3).

**Multiply:** Whites go transparent; however, all midtone is nonexistent (see Figure 2.4).

**FIGURE 2.3** The results of darkening.        **FIGURE 2.4** The results of multiplying.

**Color Burn:**    Whites go transparent; however, greater saturation occurs where midtones were present (see Figure 2.5).

**Linear Burn:**    Whites go transparent with a truer representation of the gradient (see Figure 2.6).

**FIGURE 2.5**    The results of color burn.

**FIGURE 2.6**    The results of linear burn.

## Section 2

**Lighten:**    Blacks go transparent; however, some residual midtone persists (see Figure 2.7).

**Screen:**    Blacks go transparent; however, all midtones are nonexistent (see Figure 2.8).

**FIGURE 2.7**   The results of lighten mode.    **FIGURE 2.8**   The results of screen.

**Color Dodge:**   Blacks go transparent; however, greater brightness occurs where midtones were present (see Figure 2.9).

**Linear Dodge:**   Blacks go transparent with a truer representation of the gradient (see Figure 2.10).

**FIGURE 2.9**    The result of color dodge.

**FIGURE 2.10**    The result of linear dodge.

## Section 3

**Overlay:**    Midtones go transparent with some increased saturation in the low tones and higher brightness in the high tones (see Figure 2.11).

**Soft Light:**    Midtones go transparent with subtle saturation in the low tones and subtle increased brightness in the high tones (see Figure 2.12).

**FIGURE 2.11**    The result of overlay.

**FIGURE 2.12**    The result of applying soft light.

**Hard Light:**    Midtones go transparent with higher dominance of black and white (see Figure 2.13).

**Vivid Light:**    Midtones go transparent with drastic dominance of black and white (see Figure 2.14).

**FIGURE 2.13**   The result of applying hard light.

**FIGURE 2.14**   The result of applying vivid light.

**Linear Light:**   Midtones go transparent with purer representation of the whites and blacks (see Figure 2.15).

**Pin Light:**   Midtones go transparent with truer representation of the gradient (see Figure 2.16).

**FIGURE 2.15**   The result of applying linear light.

**FIGURE 2.16**   The result of applying pin light.

**Hard Mix:**   Midtones go transparent with a posterizing effect (see Figure 2.17).

As your work through the tutorials you will be given some practical applications of the use of blend modes. There are no rules about creativity. Just set your mind to achieving more dynamic results.

**FIGURE 2.17**    The result of applying hard mix.

## PHOTOSHOP'S NATIVE 8-BIT ENVIRONMENT

The key to mastering Photoshop is mastering selections. Selections, masks, and channels are identical.

The image shown in Figure 2.18 is the key to how Photoshop manages image editing.

**FIGURE 2.18**    Gradient of 256 shades of gray.

That's right. We are working in an 8-bit environment composed of 256 shades of gray. Let's explore this concept.

## Step 1

At the base of your Tools bar, single click on the foreground color to access your color dialog box (as shown in Figure 2.19).

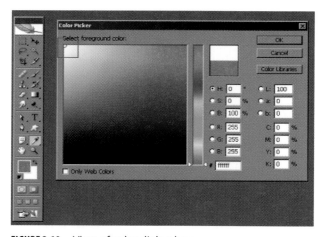

**FIGURE 2.19**    View of color dialog box.

As you click and drag the color palette mouse, the top preview swatch changes to reflect the color you select. This gives you a comparison to the original foreground color shown underneath it.

## Step 2

Place your mouse on the top left-hand corner of the color dialog box and slowly drag the mouse vertically making sure it remains on the left edge. What happens to the preview swatch?

The colors should show the range of 256 shades of gray from absolute white or luminance at the top left-hand corner until you reach absolute black or density, as shown in Figures 2.20 and 2.21. In essence, this is where all of the grays reside devoid of hue or color.

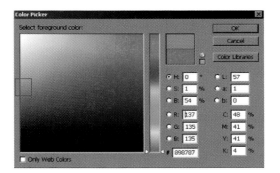

**FIGURE 2.20**    View of 256 shades of gray along the middle of the left edge.

**FIGURE 2.21**    View of 256 shades of gray along the bottom of the left edge.

## Step 3

Now place your mouse on the top left-hand corner of the color dialog box and slowly drag the mouse horizontally making sure it remains on the top edge. What happens this time?

The colors should show the range of 256 shades of hue from absolute white or luminance at the top left-hand corner until you reach absolute saturation of the single hue that is selected on the top right-hand corner. In this case, the hue is red. In essence, this is where your luminance and pure hue reside devoid of density. Figures 2.22 through 2.24 show a sample of this progression.

**FIGURE 2.22**    View of luminance and hue along the top horizontal edge.

**FIGURE 2.23**    Progression of luminance and hue along the top horizontal edge.

**FIGURE 2.24**    Resulting view of luminance and hue along the top horizontal edge.

## Step 4

Now place your mouse on the top right-hand corner of the color dialog box to get your total saturation of hue and slowly drag your mouse down making sure it remains along the right edge.

The colors should show the range of absolute saturation blended with 256 shades of density until it ends at black. Figures 2.25 through 2.27 show a sample of the progression.

Next, drag your mouse anywhere inside the color dialog box and notice that you are accessing a combination of hue, density, and luminance (see Figure 2.28).

**FIGURE 2.25**    View of saturation to density.

**FIGURE 2.26**    Progression of saturation to density.

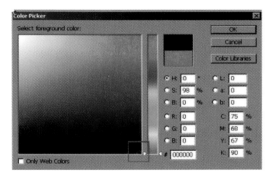

**FIGURE 2.27**    Resulting view of saturation to density.

**FIGURE 2.28**    View of hue, density, and luminance combinations.

## DEMYSTIFYING THE 8-BIT ENVIRONMENT

Photoshop CS2 allows you to view 8-, 16- and 32-bit images. The functions and tools are completely available to you in the 8-bit mode; 16- and 32-bit images will have limited capabilities.

### Step 1

Look at the numerical equivalents on the right in the color dialog box: zero for red, green, and blue is absolute black. So type 0 in each box next to the RGB boxes as shown in Figure 2.29

Notice that the small selection circle jumps to the bottom left.

**FIGURE 2.29**  Numerical equivalents for black.

## Step 2

If zero for the RGB values is absolute black and if there are only 256 shades of gray, then the numerical equivalent of absolute white is 255.

Type 255 into each box next to the RGB boxes, as shown in Figure 2.30.

Notice that the small selection circle jumps to the top left.

## Step 3

Now let's establish what the midtone will be. This is the tone that photographers worship because it gives them accurate light meter readings when they record their imagery. It is normally referred to as the 18% gray value. This value is in the middle of your absolute white and black values.

Type 128 in each box next to the RGB boxes as shown in Figure 2.31.

**FIGURE 2.30**  Numerical equivalents for white.

**FIGURE 2.31**  Numerical equivalents for medium gray.

## Step 4

Now let's get a white that is brighter than 255 white. Type 256 in the RGB boxes.

We have an error. What happened?

We just proved that Photoshop does not understand anything beyond 256 steps of gray because it's an 8-bit environment. Mathematically, that is two to the power of eight. Two multiplied by itself eight times is 256. It is base two because the computer only understands two variables: ones and zeroes (see Figure 2.32).

**FIGURE 2.32**    Error dialogue box.

## Understanding Selections

The key to mastering Photoshop is mastering selections. Selections, masks, and channels are identical.

We must keep in mind that Photoshop does not know what we are trying to achieve. We must tell it what, when, where, and how to apply its effects. This is done through selections. Let's prove this concept.

By accessing the Magic Wand tool, a selection was made around the foreground stone, as shown in Figure 2.33. Adjust your tolerance as needed. The higher the tolerance number, the greater the range of color or tone it will select. The lower the number, the less sensitive it will be in selecting tones.

As you notice, we now have what is affectionately called *marching ants*. This is our selection. Our program is communicating that any areas outside the borders of these marching ants will not respond to any of Photoshop's commands or tools.

As an example, if you apply the Hue/Saturation command while the selection is still active, all of its effects will be applied within the selected area only. In fact, all areas outside of the selection have been masked off, which supports the concept that masks and selections are the same. This approach gives us flexibility when choosing localized areas to apply Photoshop's commands or tools, as shown in Figures 2.34 and 2.35.

**FIGURE 2.33**   Selecting with the Magic Wand marquee tool.

**FIGURE 2.34**   Applying a command to the selected area.

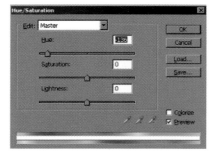

**FIGURE 2.35**   Hue/Saturation applied to selected area.

## SAVING SELECTIONS

If we work diligently to create our selections then it is a good idea to have the ability to save them. Photoshop gives us that ability. Because we are about to modify a selection, we will access the Select menu to save it to the file (Select > Save Selection). Notice that our dialog box gives us the option to name our marching ants. If we would like to gain access to our selection again then let's discover where to retrieve it.

This is where we make the connection to an often intimidating area of Photoshop called the Channels palette. Make sure that your Channels are visible (Windows > Channels) and look at the thumbnail at the bottom, as shown in Figure 2.36. Does it look familiar?

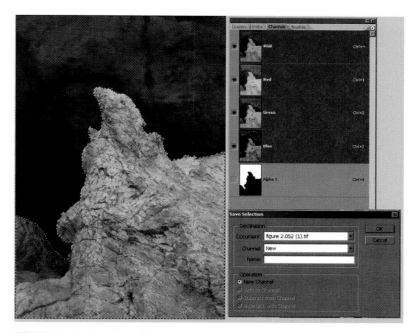

**FIGURE 2.36**     Saving the selection to create an alpha channel.

Our selection has become an additional channel called an alpha channel to our original RGB color channels. So it is important to understand that when selections are saved they go straight to channels. Now let's look a bit further.

If we can save a selection into channels, then sometimes we will need to recall them. So how do we bring our selection back again? We could activate our Load Selection command (Select > Load Selection). If you select the channel drop-down menu, you will see a list of our alpha channels, as shown in Figure 2.37.

In this case, we have only one. Notice that our marching ants are once again loaded into our document. The shortcut for loading our channels as a selection is simply to Ctrl-click on the channel itself.

## Editing Our Alpha Channel

This mask is nothing more than an image made up of 256 shades of gray. In fact, we have the ability to create selections that will have 256 levels of effects. If that is true then we should be able to paint directly on the mask for altering its form. Let's try it.

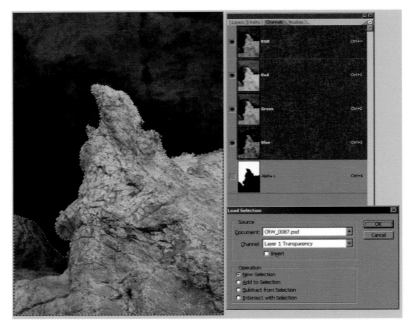

**FIGURE 2.37**    Loading the selection from an alpha channel.

If we access our paintbrush tool and make sure that our foreground color is white, we can alter the image by painting directly on the alpha channel itself, as shown in Figures 2.38 and 2.39.

All of the areas in white represent the selected content. Hit Ctrl-I to inverse the tones so that the foreground stone is selected (see Figure 2.40).

**FIGURE 2.38**    Unedited alpha channel.

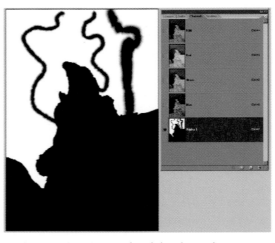

**FIGURE 2.39**    Painting on the alpha channel.

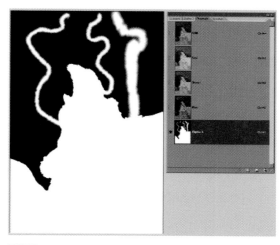

FIGURE 2.40    Tones are inversed on the alpha channel.

If we load this as a selection (Ctrl-click on the mask) we can now view what our marching ants will look like (see Figure 2.41).

Just as before, we can apply Photoshop's commands and tools to this selected area (see Figure 2.42).

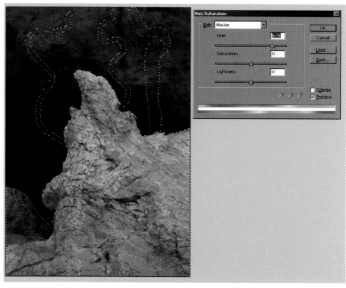

FIGURE 2.41    Loading our work as a selection.

FIGURE 2.42    Changing the newly selected area.

## LAYER MASKS DEMYSTIFIED

Now that we have gained some insight into the uses of selections, let's look at some of its more important applications. Let's delve into their uses in creating layer masks. To understand layer masks let's make sure that we understand the creative necessity of layers.

One of the most widely used aspects of Photoshop is its ability to integrate gracefully almost any unlimited amount of imagery with the use of layers. What are layers? Let's go back before the advent of digital and discover how the concept of layers was originally applied.

Let's say that your artwork was to be produced for the front cover of a magazine. The publisher's graphic department had to place the title as well as any graphic effects on the artwork. The artists did not apply the graphics to the art directly, but instead they laid over it a clear sheet of acetate and on that they placed the title of the magazine. In turn, they placed another sheet of clear acetate on top and on it they created the border graphic effects. In registration, they generated the final copy from which they produced the color separations for the magazine cover.

On a creative level, layers are important because we can apply all of Photoshop's commands and tools to each object independently from the entire scene. Placing most of the elements on separate layers gives us control and flexibility. Once the layers are established we can apply layer masking to control how each object blends and integrates into the entire image.

Layer masking is an excellent way to control the opacity or transparency of local elements in an image. Traditionally this process was done by sandwiching a litho negative with a color transparency. Sections of the litho negative were clear to allow the enlarger to expose the original image. Other sections of the negative were black, which blocked out the visual aspects on the transparency as shown in Figure 2.43. The two in registration (complete alignment), as shown in Figure 2.44, were placed into a photographic enlarger so that the image showing through the clear portion of the litho negative was exposed onto the photographic media. How do we achieve this in Photoshop?

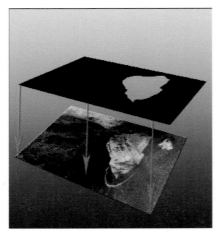

**FIGURE 2.43**    The black portions of the negative block out our view of the transparency.

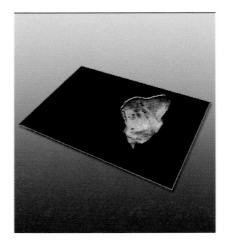

**FIGURE 2.44**    Two images in registration.

## CREATING THE LAYER MASKS

### Step 1

ON THE CD

Open an image in Photoshop and duplicate the original layer. This example uses an image of a boulder composition on the beach. You can find this image in the `Tutorials/ch 2 original images/boulder.jpg` on the CD-ROM. The foreground stone was selected using the Magic Wand selection tool and saved as an alpha channel (Select > Save Selection). Access your Channel palette (Windows > Channels). To see the alpha channel in combinations with the image as you edit the channel hit the "\" key and the areas that represent the black pixels on the channel will go to a transparent red (see Figure 2.45).

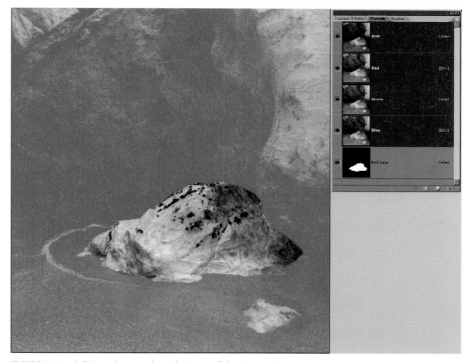

**FIGURE 2.45**    Editing the mask with view of the layers image.

If you paint with black, the red is added to the mask and if you paint with white the red is cleared from the mask. After you are done editing the mask, hit the "\" key again to get the alpha channel back to the normal black and white mode. Next, Ctrl-click on that channel to convert it to a selection.

## Step 2

Make sure that your top layer is selected and associate a layer mask by clicking on the icon that is second from the left on the bottom of the Layers palette. We apply Curves to alter the selected region's tonality, as shown in Figure 2.46.

## Step 3

Adjust Curves to see the possibilities of using it as an adjustment layer. Figures 2.47 through 2.49 show some examples of what can be achieved.

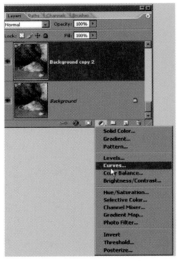

**FIGURE 2.46**   Associating a Curves adjustment layer.

**FIGURE 2.47**   Adjusting the midtones using the Curves adjustment layer.

**FIGURE 2.48**   Increasing the contrast using the Curves adjustment layer.

**FIGURE 2.49**   Decreasing the contrast using the Curves adjustment layer.

## FURTHER UNDERSTANDING OF MASKS

Earlier we learned that if we save a selection it will become an alpha channel and from that we can convert the alpha channel into a selection. If this is the case, then the same can be done to the RGB channels. Let's try.

### Step 1

ON THE CD

Open the `lone tree.jpg` (see Figure 2.50) from the CD-ROM in `Tutortials/ch 2 original images`.

**FIGURE 2.50**    View of Lone Tree.jpg

### Step 2

Let's take a look at all the channels to get a better understanding of what they are and the type of information that is inherent in each one.

Click on the red channel to view it on the canvas. If you placed black-and-white film into your camera and placed a red filter over the lens of the camera, the resulting black-and-white print would look like Figure 2.51. Notice that this channel has a greater range of contrast than the other two. This is the one that harbors all of the contrast in your digital image.

**FIGURE 2.51** Red channel view.

Next, click on the green channel.

If you placed black-and-white film into your camera and placed a green filter over the lens of the camera, the resulting black-and-white print would look like the green channel. If you look further, the contrast is the least for this channel because it is the one that contains all of the continuous midtone information (see Figure 2.52).

**FIGURE 2.52** Green channel view.

Finally, if you placed black-and-white film into your camera and placed a blue filter over the lens of the camera, the resulting black-and-white print would look like the blue channel. This is the channel that is most sensitive to the ultraviolet range of light, thus capturing much of the noise in the atmosphere. If we were to produce a black-and-white print then the blue channel would usually be the least desirable to use (see Figure 2.53).

**FIGURE 2.53**    Blue channel view.

Now let's make the connections between selection and channels.

## Step 3

Go to the Layers palette and create a new layer and fill it with black (Edit > Fill > Fill with Black). When done, click on the eyeball symbol on the left of the layer to turn it off temporarily so that you can view the channels of the tree (see Figure 2.54).

**FIGURE 2.54**    New layer filled with black.

## Step 4

Access the Channels palette and Ctrl-click on the red channel to produce a selection. With your marching ants still selected, turn on the layer filled with black. You should have something that looks similar to Figure 2.55.

**FIGURE 2.55** Creating a selection from the red channel.

## Step 5

With your marching ants still selected, turn on the layer filled with black. You should have something that looks like Figure 2.56.

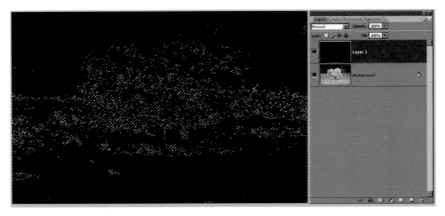

**FIGURE 2.56** Selection from the red channel over black layer.

## Step 6

Now fill the layer with white (Edit > Fill > Fill with White) and take a look at what you have (see Figure 2.57 and 2.58 for the result).

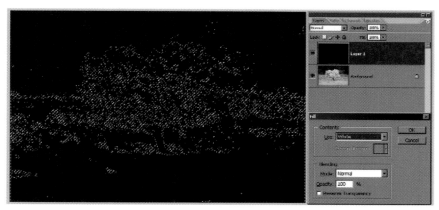

**FIGURE 2.57**    Fill selection dialog box.

Do you see what has happened? You have just transferred the red channel into a layer via a selection. As we have noted, the key to mastering Photoshop is mastering selections. Selections, masks, and channels are identical.

**FIGURE 2.58**    Results of filling the selection with white.

Now let's take this one step further and use the results to enhance the image.

## Step 7

Change the blend mode of the top layer to Screen. This will give you a nice fluffy white for the flower pedals. Everything else looks fine as is, so we will restrict the effect to the flower detail (see Figure 2.59).

**FIGURE 2.59** Layer blend mode set to Screen.

## Step 8

Notice that you have an extra white thumbnail connected to your image. This is the Layer Mask, as shown in Figure 2.60. You can paint with 256 shades of gray on this, but make sure that you click on the mask first to tell the program that you are interested in editing the mask. Photoshop is telling you that if you paint within this area with white you will be allowed to view the image that it is associated with (in this case the tree image that you set) to a Screen blend mode. If you paint with black you will mask out the object; in effect, it will disappear. Make sure that you click on the mask and fill it with black (Edit > Fill > Fill with black).

**FIGURE 2.60** Associating a layer mask.

## Step 9

Next, you are going to start working as a painter. Activate your paintbrush and use a low opacity setting to apply white paint to the filled black mask. However, you will want to apply only to the white flowers to bring out the creamy luminance that will make this image a little more dynamic, as shown in Figure 2.61.

Alt-click on the mask to view it in the canvass area, as shown in Figure 2.62.

Now that we have an understanding of selections, mask, and layer blending modes, let's move on to apply our knowledge to some creative applications.

**FIGURE 2.61**    Editing the layer mask.

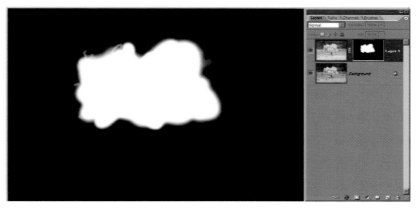

**FIGURE 2.62**    Mask viewed on canvass.

## USING CHANNELS TO MAKE MASKS

Let's look at another option for creating masks. Click on each channel to understand its properties.

The red channel harbors the contrast of your image. Let's relate this to photography before the advent of digital. If you photographed this image using black-and-white film and placed a red filter over the lens and then proceeded to make a black-and-white print, then this channel is what the print would look like (see Figure 2.63).

**FIGURE 2.63**    View of the red channel.

The green channel harbors the continuous midtone grays in your image. If you photographed this image using black-and-white film and placed a green filter over the lens and then proceeded to make a black-and-white print, then this channel is what the print would look like (see Figure 2.64).

The blue channel harbors the noise from the atmosphere. This is the channel that is more sensitive to ultraviolet radiation. The same comparison pertains to this channel as well, in that if you photographed this image using a blue filter over the lens, the black-and-white print would resemble this channel (see Figure 2.65).

We are going to make a mask revealing the whites of the blossoms. There is an advantage to creating a mask this way because your channels already contain all of the textural details of your image in shades of gray, therefore, you can create a more accurate mask. In fact, with much practice you could create mask faster this way. Let's continue.

**FIGURE 2.64**    View of the green channel.

**FIGURE 2.65**    View of the blue channel.

## Step 1

View each of your channels and determine which one will give you the best tonal separation between the blossoms on the tree and the background. In this case the blue channel works the best. You do not want to alter the original channel because this will alter the blue hues in the image, so create a duplicate of it to create an alpha channel. By default it will be named Blue copy. You will use this to create your mask (see Figure 2.66).

**FIGURE 2.66**    View of blue channel copy.

## Step 2

Hit Ctrl-M for Curves and Ctrl-click on the gray grass located next to the blossom to place a point on the section of the graph that represents the selected tonality (see Figure 2.67).

**FIGURE 2.67**    Place point of the Curve representing the background details.

## Step 3

Now do the same thing for the white blossom to place a point on the section of the graph that represents its selected tonality. Now that you have the two tonalities mapped, you can create some extreme contrast to make the blossoms white and the background details black (see Figure 2.68).

**FIGURE 2.68**    Place point of the Curve representing the white blossoms.

## Step 4

Take the point that represents the background detail and drag it to the lower extremity to send the selected midgrays to black. Do the same for the blossoms and send that point upwards to send its tones to pure white (see Figure 2.69).

**FIGURE 2.69**    Create extreme contrast using the mapped points.

## Step 5

The last step is to use the Paintbrush to paint any unwanted details black leaving only the blossom detail (see Figure 2.70).

**FIGURE 2.70**    Edit the mask with the Paintbrush.

Now that you have the mask you can apply it to the layer that has the Screen blend mode. Ctrl-click on the Blue copy alpha channel to get your selection. Now add a layer mask and notice that the alpha channel has been transferred to the mask. In essence the selections were honored so that the areas selected remain white and everything else is masked out with black, as shown in Figure 2.71.

**FIGURE 2.71**    Apply alpha channel as a layer mask.

Now that we have an understanding of selections, mask, and layer blending modes let's move on and apply our knowledge to some creative applications.

## What You Have Learned

- How and why layer blend modes work the way they do
- The key to mastering Photoshop is mastering selections. Selections, masks, and channels are identical
- You are working optimally in 8 bits
- How to create and edit alpha channels to create layer masks
- How to create masks from alpha channels

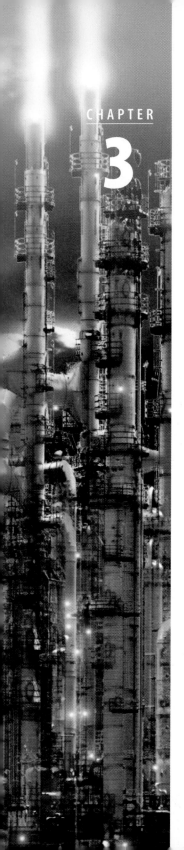

# USING HDR AND SMART OBJECTS TO COMPOSITE PHOTOS

**IN THIS CHAPTER**

- Powerful approaches to compositing photographic imagery
- Practical use of the new HDR Merge
- Introduction to the new Smart Objects
- How to use layer sets to organize your work
- How to use Layer Blending modes to assist with composition
- The power of the Free Transform and Distort for localized areas
- Practical applications to using layer masks
- Creating masks from channels
- The usefulness of third-party filters to enhance your creations

## USING PHOTOGRAPHS AS A CREATIVE MEDIUM

The purpose of this exercise is to give you an insight into the possibilities of what one photographic image can do if you allow your mind to be open to alternative ways of seeing. Why honor the single shot if you can show something with a more interesting twist?

Most photographers compose for a single expressive image. This technique has been widely used because of the level of difficulty of achieving successful image blends in the traditional darkroom. It could be done, but not without a series of enlargers with an impeccable registration system to ensure that the images were exposed and placed properly for a seamless integration. Now we have the advantage of the digital darkroom.

We will use two different photographs in this chapter: a sunset and a photo of a processing plant. We will start by building the backdrop using a series of exposures of a single image to achieve a greater dynamic range using the new HDR Merge (High Dynamic Range).

The problem with digital cameras is that you are limited to 8 bits of information. If you have seen a well-printed black-and-white print such as an Ansel Adams print, then you know that the brilliance of his photographs comes not only from his skill as a photograher and visionary, but also from the ability of the silver in the negatives and papers to render an infinite range of grays. Adams was able to produce work with an extremely wide range of tonal grays and manipulate them to his artistic vision.

Most current digital cameras work optimally with a maximum range of 256 shades of gray. HDR Merge provides a workaround that ensures that you have proper information in the shadows and the highlights using a series of bracketed images, and allows you to extend the amount of tonal information in a single file to 32 bits. In fact, the final file can be exported in either 8 bits, 16 bits or 32 bits.

That is the technical part of this exercise. Next, we will create the main subject in the foreground using a series of duplicates of the processing plant. However, you will give it a little different creative spin. Let's begin.

### Step 1

ON THE CD

Open Adobe Bridge (File > Browse) and navigate the CD-ROM that comes with this book to the `Tutorials/ch 3 industrial`.

Bridge will give you a thumbnail of all of the images in this folder. Select `sunset 001.tif` to `sunset 005.tif`, as shown in Figure 3.1.

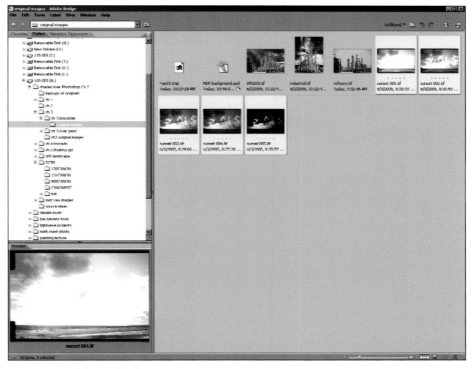

**FIGURE 3.1**    Adobe Bridge layout.

### Step 2

In the Adobe Bridge menu select Tools > Photoshop > Merge to HDR.

## Step 3

The images that are about to be merged were scanned with a Nikon 8000 at one-stop exposure increments, meaning each one was given double the exposure of the previous, which can give a nice 4000 ppi scan. If these images were taken with a digital camera you would not get the Manually Set EV dialog box, as shown in Figure 3.2. The HDR Merge command does not understand what exposures were used with each of these images because they were scanned with a professional scanner and there is no metadata embedded in the files. Most scanners do not embed aperture and shutter speeds since none are used in the creation of the digital file. So the program asks you to organize the exposure hierarchy manually.

**FIGURE 3.2**    Manually Set EV dialog box.

## Step 4

Each file was given a one-stop exposure adjustment with the exception of sunset 005.tif, which was given two stops less exposure from sunset 004.tif. This was done to favor more details in the highlights. In essence, the shaded areas will look very dark but the brighter areas will have the texture and detail that is appealing for sunset shots. Set the shutter speeds to reflect 1 stop increments.

When finished click OK.

## Step 5

You should now see the main HDR interface where you can make adjustments to merge the high and low tones. The greatest issue with 8-bit images is the lack of dynamic range. In other words, the lack of the current camera's ability to record a large number of colors and tones. This interface allows us to fake the process of gaining greater dynamic range. By recording a series of images that will record extreme shadow detail as shown in sunset 001.tif toward images that give you great detail in the highlights as shown in sunset 005.tif, Merge to HDR will merge all of the images in such a way that you will not lose detail in either the shadow or highlight regions.

On your left you will see the series of images that you loaded in. The center preview image is the result of the merged data. The histogram allows you to make subtle adjustments as well

Above the histogram you have the option to allow it to export the file as an 8-bit, 16-bit, or 32-bit format. Select the 32-bit option so that you can maintain as much information as possible when you commit your changes (see Figure 3.3).

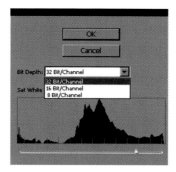

**FIGURE 3.3**    Bit depth options.

## Step 6

Uncheck the top image to see what happens. Because you deselected the image that supplied most of the luminosity, the preview goes slightly darker (see Figure 3.4A & B).

## Step 7

Reselect the top image and deselect the last one to see what happens. Did you see the preview go brighter? Because you deselected the image that supplied most of the density the preview went brighter (see Figure 3.4B).

## Step 8

Now deselect both the first and the last image properties to see the outcome. Notice that with both extremes uninvolved, the resulting preview is dominated with mostly midtones and brighter values (see Figure 3.5A).

**FIGURE 3.4**    A) First view is deselected. B) Last view is deselected.

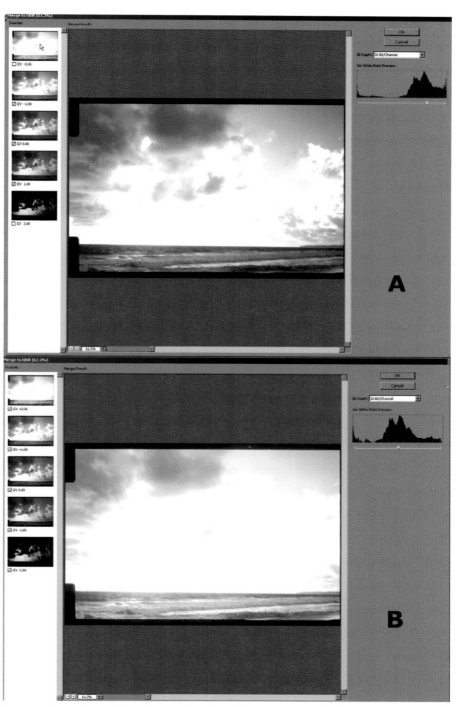

**FIGURE 3.5**    A) First and last view are deselected. B) Last view is deselected.

## Step 9

Make sure that all of the thumbnails are selected and focus on the histogram to the right. Slowly move the slider to the left so that you can see where the tonal information of the image is shifted (see Figure 3.5B).

Next, move the slider to the right and notice how the tones are shifted to the lower tonalities, as shown in Figure 3.6.

**FIGURE 3.6**    Tonal information of the image is shifted.

The richer result works great for the background since you are trying to portray depth, so click OK.

## Step 10

Change the image to 8 bits by accessing Image > Mode > 8 bit. You will see the HDR Conversion panel, as shown in Figure 3.7, that will give you options for making subtle contrast adjustments before it converts the file to 8 bits of information. It is necessary to alter the file to 8 bits of information because most of Photoshop's functions are not available in 32-bit mode. So make sure that you save your file under a different name like "sunset 8bit" to preserve your original 32-bit file. Printers and software packages are quickly adapting to the need for higher dynamic range, so think toward the future and save as much information as possible.

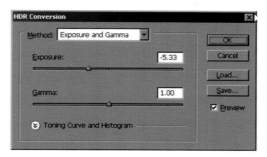

**FIGURE 3.7**    HDR Conversion panel.

The controls seem limited at first, giving you only Exposure and Gama compensations, but look at the lower left-hand corner and notice another option called Toning Curve and Histogram, as shown in Figure 3.8. Click on the drop arrows to view additional editing options. You now have the histogram in combination with Curves. You also have a visual layout of the 256 shades of gray listed in the lower window, representing absolute black to absolute white. Take a look at the higher tones of gray and notice that the mound in the graph is much higher above those grays. The higher the mound, the more information exists for that particular gray.

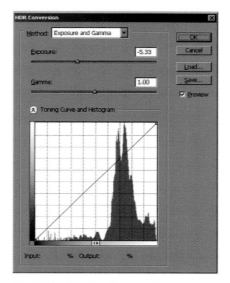

**FIGURE 3.8**    Toning Curve options.

By clicking on the diagonal line you will apply a point that you will drag to make changes to any of the grays in your image. If you shift higher they will become brighter and if you shift lower they will become darker.

*Remember: it is necessary to alter the file to 8 bits of information because most of Photoshop's functions are not available in 32-bit mode.*

In the expanded view you have the curves that are related to several presets under the menu called Method. Click on the drop-down menu and view each setting. Exposure and Gamma is the first option available to you (Figure 3.9A). Highlight Compensation shifts the tones to favor brighter highlights, as shown in Figure 3.9B. Equalize Histogram balances the tones to favor acceptable highlight and shadow detail (see Figure 3.9C).

Unlike the other presets, the Local Adaptation allows you to edit the curve to achieve the tonal results of your choice. Figure 3.9D shows the results of the preset before you make changes to it.

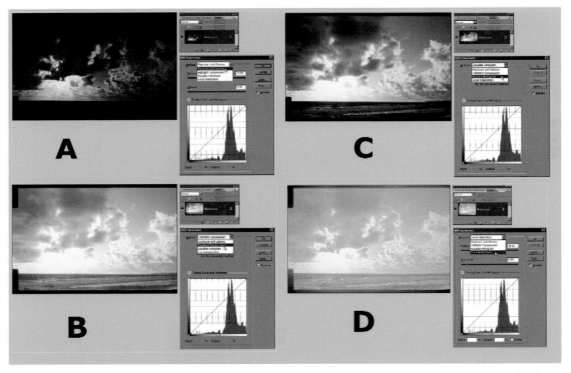

**FIGURE 3.9**    A) Exposure and Gamma. B) View of Highlight Compensation. C) View Equalize Histogram. D) View of Local Adaptation.

### Step 11

Add points by clicking on the curve just as if you were working in the Curves command and adjust the tonal information in the image to your liking (see Figure 3.10).

This example keeps as much detail in the highlights as possible and allows the midtones to take on a rich tonality to prevent the sky from competing with the foreground image.

### Step 12

To make editing a little easier, use the Crop tool to select the cloud formation and discard the black border (see Figure 3.11).

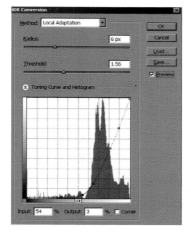

**FIGURE 3.10**    Click on the curve to adjust the tonal information.

**FIGURE 3.11**    Final results after cropping.

## CREATING THE FOREGROUND

It's time to start creating the foreground structure. This is where you will take one image and composite multiple copies to produce a much more interesting structure than the original.

### Step 1

*ON THE CD*

Using Bridge (File > Browse), navigate to the `Tutorials` folder on the CD-ROM, access the `ch 3 industrial` subfolder, and open `sunset architecture.tif`.

### Step 2

The first step is to create a mask so that the sky will go transparent and the structure remains. You will do this with the aid of your channels (Windows > Channels). Click on each channel, to view their tonal properties and determine which one will give you the best tonal separation between the foreground and the sky.

### Step 3

After inspecting your channels, it's obvious that the blue channel gives the best results, so duplicate this one by clicking and dragging it on top of the new channels icon, which is located to the left of the garbage can symbol on the bottom of your Channels palette.

### Step 4

Access Curves (Image > Adjustments > Curves) to begin editing the tones in your image. The goal is to separate the tones so that the background is completely white and the foreground structure is solid black. From this you will create your mask. Place your mouse on the sky and Ctrl-click. This action places a dot on the curve that represents the position of that tone.

Next, place your mouse on the pipe region and Ctrl-click. This action places a dot on the curve that represents that midtone position (see Figure 3.12).

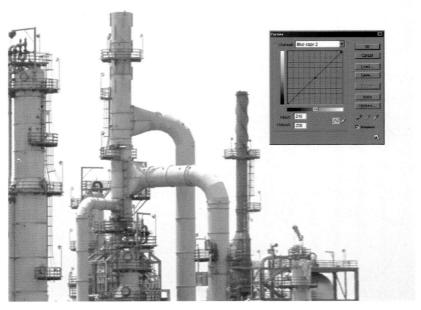

**FIGURE 3.12**    Midtones are established on the curves.

## Step 5

Start with the center dot and pull it straight down to the base to alter all of the mid-tone information into black.

Do the same for the highlights by dragging the top dot all the way up, and as a result, the highlights will change to white (see Figure 3.13).

**FIGURE 3.13**    Midtones changed to black and highlights are brightened.

## Step 6

Use Levels (Image Adjustments > Levels) to fine-tune your mask further, as shown in Figure 3.14. Don't forget to use your paintbrush to edit the mask to completion if needed. There are no rules to how this is done. All that you are concerned with at this stage is producing a black-and-white image that will define your sky and foreground object.

Now invert the tones by clicking Ctrl-I so that the foreground elements are selected.

*Although there are many other ways to do this, the channels will provide you with the bulk of the information that you need to mask your shapes. So be patient; as you practice this approach it will become a fast process.*

Ctl-click on your new mask to convert it into a selection. Next, make sure that you are in the Layers palette (Windows > Layers) and click the Create Layer Mask button, which is the third button from the left on the bottom of your Layers palette. This will create a mask to isolate the background (see Figure 3.15).

**FIGURE 3.14** Completed mask.

**FIGURE 3.15** Inverted tones.

## Step 7

Add Hue and Saturation, Color Balance, and Curves. Adjust the layers to shift the blue saturated image toward a warmer color image.

### Step 8

You will use the results of this layer to create the new foreground architecture. To make the process easier, merge the three adjustment layers with the image by Ctrl-clicking on the right side of all four layers to select them. Access the layers submenu and click Merge Layers.

## CREATING THE NEW ARCHITECTURE

Give the composition a vertical format.

### Step 1

Access Image > Canvas Size and resize the canvas to 7.5 inches wide and 10 inches high.

### Step 2

Starting with the merged layer duplicate it and transform the new one by stretching upward to about two-thirds of the way up into the image, as shown in Figure 3.16. Additionally, flip the canvas horizontally (Image > Rotate Canvas > Flip Horizontally).

**FIGURE 3.16**    Transform the new image by stretching upward.

### Step 3

Add a layer mask to the duplicate layer and edit out portions of the image so that the result doesn't look too repetitive (see Figure 3.17).

**FIGURE 3.17** Mask associated with the layer.

### Step 4

Duplicate the layer again but this time offset it slightly to the left, as shown in Figure 3.18.

### Step 5

Duplicate the top layer but this time change the blend mode to Hard Light (see Figure 3.19).

### Step 6

Duplicate the top layer again and change the blend mode to Overlay but this time move toward the bottom so that the peak tower appears just above the lower right-hand corner (see Figure 3.20).

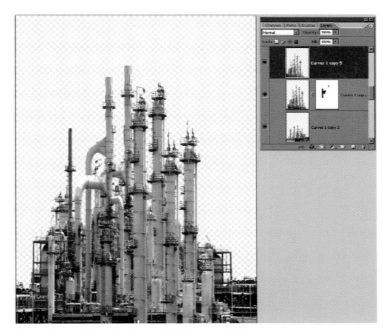

**FIGURE 3.18**    Offset the layer slightly to the left.

**FIGURE 3.19**    Duplicated layer's blend mode is set to Hard Light.

**FIGURE 3.20**    Duplicated layer's blend mode is set to Overlay.

### Step 7

*ON THE CD*

On the CD-ROM in the `Tutorials/ch 3 industrial` folder, open `background final.tif` and place it below the architecture layers so that it fills the entire background. Use the Freetransform tool to achieve this (see Figure 3.21).

### Step 8

As a result of transforming each layer there is pixel information beyond the borders of your composition and this is taxing on your RAM. Use the Crop tool to select the entire image and hit enter on your keyboard to discard any unseen imagery. This will discard the unseen pixels beyond the borders of your image and therefore save memory.

### Step 9

Next, we will give the image better perspective to aid the viewer's eye to travel from the foreground into the background. Make sure that the background sunset is still selected and give it a little perspective. Use the Pespective tool (Edit > Transform > Perspective) and drag the points on the top corners apart from one another, as shown in Figure 3.22.

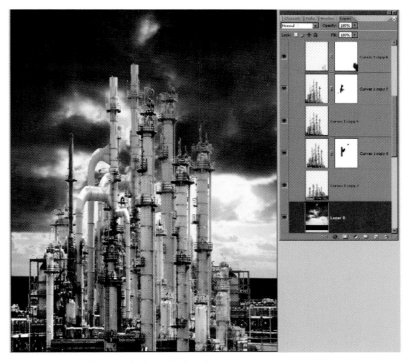

**FIGURE 3.21**    Background placed below layers.

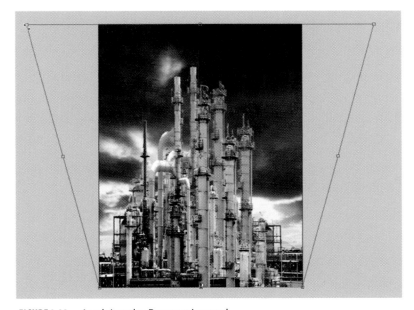

**FIGURE 3.22**    Applying the Perspective tool.

## Step 10

*ON THE CD*

On the CD-ROM open the `Tutorials/ch 3 industrial/clouds.tif` and place it above the background sunset layer. Next, change the blend mode to Multiply (see Figure 3.23).

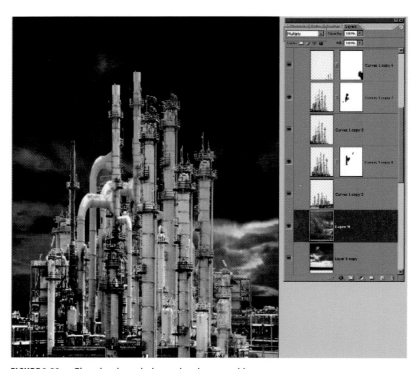

**FIGURE 3.23**    Clouds placed above background layers.

## Step 11

The darker tones in the cloud image now dominate the background, giving the brighter region a little more detail and interest. However, the effect makes the top region a little muddy visually, so we restrict the effect of this layer by adding a gradient mask. To accomplish this, add a standard layer mask and make sure it is selected. Access your gradient tool (G) and hit the D key on your keyboard to make the foreground color black and the background color white. Place your mouse on the top edge of your canvas and hold the Shift key to restrict the effect to one axis. Now drag your tool to the bottom edge of your page and release the mouse. Your gradient mask will allow a subtle transition from no effect at the top portion of your background to the complete effect of the cloud layer in multiply mode (see Figure 3.24).

You can fine-tune your mask with the Levels command to restrict the span of the gradient (see Figure 3.25).

**FIGURE 3.24**    Adding a gradient mask.

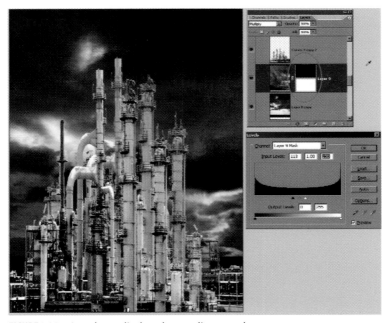

**FIGURE 3.25**    Levels applied to the gradient mask.

## ADDING LIGHTS TO ARCHITECTURE

Now we will add some life to the refinery by adding structure lights and lighting details.

### Step 1

Start by creating a new layer and filling it with medium gray (Edit > Fill > Fill with 50% Gray).

### Step 2

Apply a Lens Flare of your choice to the medium gray layer and change the blend mode to Hardlight.

### Step 3

On the bottom of your Layers palette, click the third icon from the right to create a layer group. Call this set "flares." Highlight the flares layer set and create another called "reds." This one will appear inside the flares layer set. Now drag your lens flare layer into the reds folder (see Figure 3.26).

**FIGURE 3.26**   Placing the Lens Flare.

## Step 4

Free Transform (Edit > Free Transform) the Lens Flare and place along the side of one of the towers, as shown in Figure 3.27.

**FIGURE 3.27**    Lens Flare transformed.

## Step 5

Hold down the Alt key and with your Move tool selected, drag to duplicate the Lens Flare. Repeat the process and place Lens Flares throughout different locations of the architecture. All of the duplicated layers will appear in the reds layer set.

## Step 6

Merge all of the Lens Flares into one layer by selecting all of the duplicate layers. Access the Layers submenu and click Merge Layers. After they are merged make sure to change the blend mode back to Hardlight (see Figures 3.28 and 3.29).

## Step 7

Now we will create the fiery smoke extending to the sky. Follow Steps 1 and 2 to create another Lens Flare. Use Free Transform to stretch the Lens Flare upward (Figure 3.30).

## Step 8

Let's give it some motion and softness by adding some motion blur (Filter > Blur > Motion Blur), as shown in Figure 3.31.

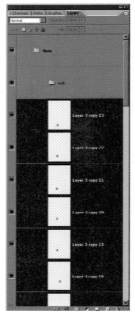

**FIGURE 3.28**  Lens Flare layers highlighted.

**FIGURE 3.29**  Lens Flare layers merged.

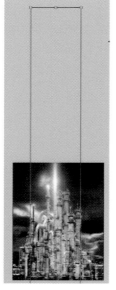

**FIGURE 3.30**  Lens Flare layers transformed.

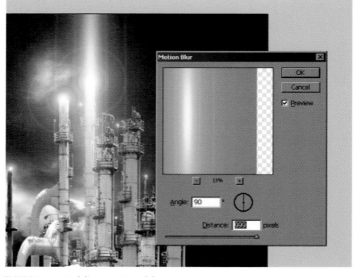

**FIGURE 3.31**  Adding motion blur.

## Step 9

Use your Perspective tool (Edit > Transform > Perspective) to distort the flare upward and out, as shown in Figure 3.32.

**FIGURE 3.32**    Distorting flare.

## Step 10

ON THE CD

In Chapter 1 you learned how to save brush palettes. Now you are going to load a custom brush palette. Activate the paintbrush and expand the brush presets to view the variety of brush styles with their thumbnail view. Click the black triangle in the top right corner and select the Load Brushes submenu. Navigate to the CD-ROM in the Tutorials/Custom Brushes and load Smoke Brushes.abr. Create a new layer above the architecture and with a low opacity of 12%, add use Smoke Brush 4 from the options bar and paint in your smoke. We will not go into how the brush preset was created here. This will be covered in detail in Chapter 4. For now just enjoy the effects of the Smoke Brush (see Figure 3.33).

**FIGURE 3.33**    Add smoke.

## GIVING THE SCENE A SENSE OF NIGHT

Creating a nighttime atmosphere for this scene not only gives it depth but also it is an opportunity to allow the tower lights to jump forward. Let's have some fun.

### Step 1

Create a new layer set that is positioned above the architecture layers but below the flares layer set. Inside it create a new layer and fill it with a rich blue of your choice.

### Step 2

Change the new layers blend mode to Color Burn to get a beautiful blue overlay with rich deep shadows (see Figure 3.34). You will need to do some editing to the blue fill, so give it a layer mask, as shown in Figure 3.35.

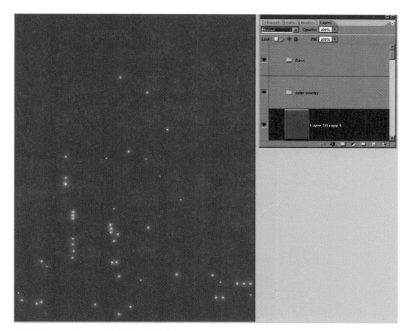

**FIGURE 3.34**   Layer filled with blue.

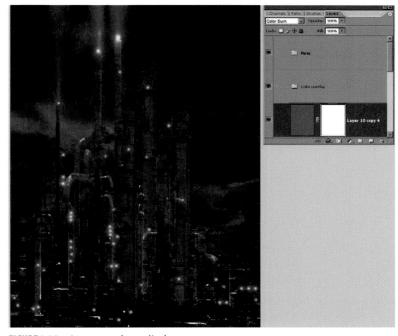

**FIGURE 3.35**   Layer mask applied.

### Step 3

The objective is to isolate the blue effect to the background. Since the architecture is on a series of layers, you will create a selection for each one for the purpose of editing the mask of the blue-filled layer. Ctrl-click on the first architecture layer to convert the object to a selection. Make sure that you are in the layer mask of the blue-filled layer, and fill the selection with black, as shown in Figure 3.36.

**FIGURE 3.36**   Layer mask edited.

### Step 4

Repeat Step 3 for all of the architecture layers. Don't forget to edit the mask with your paintbrush to fine-tune it. Figure 3.37 shows the final results of the edited mask.

 *You could also use Ctrl-shift-click on each of the layer masks to select them all and then fill the blue-filled layer with black as well.*

### Step 5

The next step is to create the blue effect for both the architecture and the background. So duplicate the blue-filled layer and invert the tones of the mask (Ctrl-I), as shown in Figure 3.38.

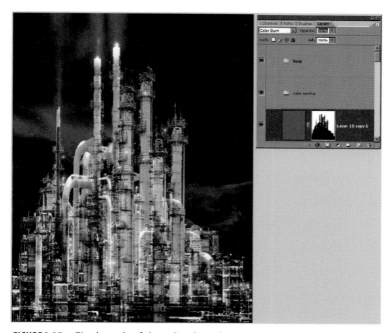

**FIGURE 3.37**   Final result of the edited mask.

**FIGURE 3.38**   Inverse the tones.

## Step 6

Select the effect for the background and reduce its opacity to 41%. Select the effect for the foreground and reduce its opacity to 30%.

## Step 7

The architecture seems a little flat so let's give it some contour. Duplicate the foreground color fill layer.

**FIGURE 3.39** Reduce the foreground opacity.

## Step 8

Apply the Minimum command (Filters > Other > Minimum) to the mask and give it a radius of 28 pixels. This will shift the black inward to expose the lighter colors around the edges of the architecture giving a rim lighting effect (see Figure 3.40).

## Step 9

The rim lighting effect is pixilated; therefore, it appears blocky around the perimeter of the architecture. We apply some Gaussian Blur (Filters > Blur > Gaussian Blur) to the mask, as shown in Figure 3.41.

**FIGURE 3.40**  Minimum applied.

**FIGURE 3.41**  Additional Gaussian Blur applied.

## Step 10

The image is taking on a more dramatic look but it could still use a little more interest. Create a new layer beneath the two blue-filled layers. Fill it with a gradient of blue to gold starting from the top to the bottom (see Figure 3.42).

**FIGURE 3.42**    Gradient Fill applied.

Click and drag the layer mask of the blue-filled layer above it and drag it while holding the Alt key on top of the new gradient-filled layer. Your gradient layer now has the layer mask used to outline the architecture.

However, you want the gradient to be isolated to the back region of your scene, so make sure that the mask is selected by clicking it once and hit Ctl-I to inverse the tones. The result should be similar to that shown in Figure 3.43.

## Step 11

Now edit the blue-filled layer's masks with the Paintbrush to allow the fiery smoke to become more prominent (see Figure 3.44).

**FIGURE 3.43**    Selection applied to Gradient Fill.

**FIGURE 3.44**    Mask applied to Gradient Fill.

## Step 12

So far everything looks great, but the rim lighting on the architecture could be a little more dynamic. We will make modifications to enhance this area.

Start by merging all of the layers that make up the architecture image into one. Select the first architecture layer and as you hold down your Shift key select the last one. You have just selected multiple layers. Now hold down your Alt key and access the layers submenu and select Merge layers. You have just merged the selected layers into a new layer without affecting the originals (see Figure 3.45).

**FIGURE 3.45**   Architecture layers merged.

## Step 13

Change this new layer's blend mode to Color Dodge (see Figure 3.46).

## Step 14

Alt-drag on the mask that was used for the gradient fill on top of the new architecture layer. Then apply the Maximum command (Filters > Other > Maximum) to the mask. Give it a radius of 8 pixels to expand the white and decrease the black (see Figure 3.47). This places a stronger highlight around the architecture.

## Step 15

As before, apply a slight Gaussian Blur to the mask to soften the effects of the Maximum filter (see Figure 3.48).

**FIGURE 3.46**   Color Dodge applied.

**FIGURE 3.47**   Maximum applied to mask.

**FIGURE 3.48**   Gaussian Blur applied to mask.

## ADDING THIRD-PARTY FILTERS

Now we will add some finishing touches to give our image a little more visual interest by using nik Color Efex Pro 2.0. nik multimedia, the company that introduced nik Sharpener, has some wonderful filters for Photoshop that cater to the photographic

community. The newest is the nik Color Efex Pro 2.0. Their filters are ideal for a situation like this one—especially for the final enhancements: the Graduated Fog and the Color Stylizer Filter. Go to the CD-ROM and install nik Sharpener 2.0 and Color Efex Pro 2.0 from the Demos folder.

*ON THE CD*

## Step 1

When it is activated, navigate to File > Automate > nik Color Efex Pro 2.0, and a panel floats over the Photoshop interface listing all of the plug-in filters alphabetically. Select Graduated Fog. Experiment with the settings and choose what you like best (see Figures 3.49 and 3.50).

**FIGURE 3.49**     Graduated Fog Panel.

**FIGURE 3.50**     Extended view of image after Step 1.

## Step 2

In addition, select Color Stylizer. Experiment with these settings as well (see Figure 3.51). Finally, nik Color Efex Pro 2.0 gives you a layer with a mask that represents the changes you made with its filter. Reduce the opacity of the Color Stylizer layer to allow some of the blue tones to come through.

With just two photographic images you are able to produce some dynamic results. Practice and experiment to come up with your own challenges.

**FIGURE 3.51**    Final view of image after Step 2.

## Composite Photography with Smart Objects

Now we will continue on with an exploration of compositing photographic imagery, but this time we will discover another new feature in Photoshop CS2 called Smart Objects. Let's start with a photograph captured in Death Valley National Park.

*ON THE CD*

### Step 1

Open a file (Ctrl-O) and navigate to the CD-ROM. Access Tutorials/ch 3 over pass/ deathvalley1.tif. Duplicate (Ctrl-J) and flip the layer horizontally (Edit > Transform > Flip Horizontal). Next, add a layer mask and block out the sky of the top layer to allow the other horizon to come through (see Figure 3.52).

*ON THE CD*

### Step 2

Open a file (Ctrl-O) and navigate to the CD-ROM. Access Tutorials/ch 3 over pass/ deathvalley2.tif and place it on top of the two landscape layers. Apply a mask to it and edit it so that the horizon does not interfere with the duplicated layers.

Eventually you will composite a bridge into this scene, so use your Rubber Stamp tool to clone out the mountain reflection. Alt-click on a portion of the water that you would like to replace the reflection, then click on the reflection to apply the new texture (see Figure 3.53).

**FIGURE 3.52**    Layer flipped and masked.

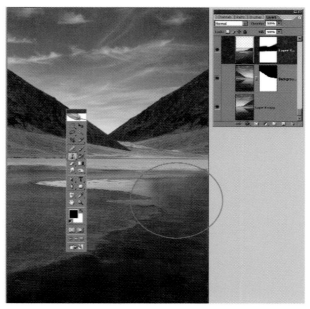

**FIGURE 3.53**    Removing the reflection.

### Step 3

Open a file (Ctrl-O) and navigate to the CD-ROM. Access `Tutorials/ch 3 over pass/ Bridge.tif`.

### Step 4

Use your Pen tool to outline the bridge with a path. You could make a Vector Mask using the current path but this will not give you the ability to edit with the Paintbrush or apply blurring effects which you might want to do later, so Ctrl-click on the path to get a selection. Follow by applying a layer mask to hide areas around the bridge (see Figure 3.54).

**FIGURE 3.54**   Bridge path created.

### Step 5

Convert the bridge layer into a Smart Object. Access the Layers submenu and select Group Into Smart Objects (see Figure 3.55).

### Step 6

Next, you are going to split up the left and right sides of the bridge into their own layers. Duplicate the bridge layer and mask out one-half of the bridge on one layer and the opposite half on the other layer (see Figures 3.56 and 3.57).

**FIGURE 3.55**    Result of bridge grouped as Smart Object.

**FIGURE 3.56**    Right bridge created.

**FIGURE 3.57** Left bridge created.

## Step 7

Turn off the visual aspects of the bridge on the right so that you are viewing only the left bridge. Let's discover Smart Objects. Figures 3.58 and 3.59 show an example of how Smart Objects function. Smart Object is a sophisticated form of the Revert command (File > Revert).

Notice that there is a symbol on the bottom right-hand corner of the layer denoting that Smart Objects are in effect. Let's do an experiment to see the advantages of Smart Objects. Transform (Ctl-T) this layer, make it small, and hit enter to commit your changes. Now transform it again, but this time enlarge it to just under the size it used to be. The original quality is maintained. Keep in mind that you do not want to enlarge the object past its original size because this will interpolate the image.

## Step 8

There will be situations where you will want to composite images that are taken at the same time of day but somehow have slight color shifts. Or maybe the surrounding environment reflects a different color of ambient light. You cannot always control the lighting and color situation. Therefore, matching the bridge to the color balance of the background, make the following changes, as shown in Figure 3.60.

**FIGURE 3.58**    Transforming Smart Object to smaller size.

**FIGURE 3.59**    Transform Smart Object to a larger size.

**FIGURE 3.60**    View of applied corrections.

### Step 9

Turn back on the visual aspects of the right bridge. The following settings are the color and tonal adjustments that we applied to the right bridge. Don't be afraid to vary these settings (see Figure 3.61).

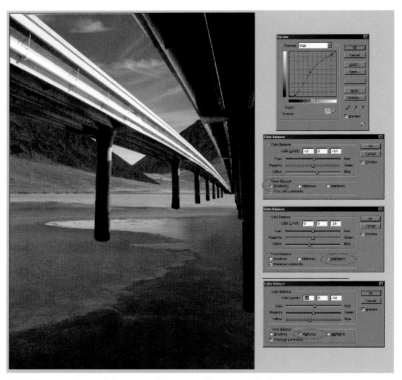

**FIGURE 3.61** Second Curves adjustment layer applied.

Next, organize your layers and create two layer sets. Call one "Left Bridge" and the other "Right Bridge." Place into them all of the layers relating to each one.

### Step 10

Create another layer group and call it "bridge reflections and shadows." Place the right and left bridge into their respective folders (see Figure 3.62).

### Step 11

Give the reflection layer a mask and edit the mask so that the bridges only show up in the water areas (see Figure 3.63).

**FIGURE 3.62** Reflection created.

**FIGURE 3.63** Reflection is masked to water locations.

## Step 12

Below the reflections add two new layers and place a shadow for the left bridge on one and a shadow for the right bridge on the other (see Figure 3.64).

**FIGURE 3.64** Bridge shadows are added.

### Step 13

Open Adobe Bridge (File > Browse) and navigate the CD-ROM that comes with this book to the `Tutorials/ch 3 over pass` and open `desert tire.tif`. Create a selection around the tire using the Pen tool.

### Step 14

Using your Move tool, place the tire above the shadow layer, and use your Free Transform Ctrl-T to flip it horizontally to match the light coming from the left, as shown in Figure 3.65.

**FIGURE 3.65**   Tire dragged into overpass scene.

### Step 15

Duplicate the tire layer and select the first one. Fill the layer with black (Edit > Fill > Fill with black). Make sure that the Preserve Transparency option is on to fill only the tire and nothing else (see Figure 3.66). Give it a Gaussian Blur and bring the layer's opacity to around 50%.

### Step 16

Using the Color Balance adjustment layer, balance the color of the tire to reflect the overall environment of the scene, as shown in Figure 3.67.

**FIGURE 3.66**    Shadow of the tire created.

**FIGURE 3.67**    Color Balance applied to the tire.

## APPLYING CONCRETE SUPPORTS

### Step 1

Each pillar underneath the bridge should have a concrete support, so let's create them from the tire image. Copy and paste an elliptical sample of the concrete as well as a rectangular sample (see Figures 3.68 and 3.69).

**FIGURE 3.68** Elliptical selection of concrete.

**FIGURE 3.69** Rectangular selection of concrete.

### Step 2

Duplicate (Ctl-J) the elliptical sample and position it to round off the base, as shown in Figure 3.70.

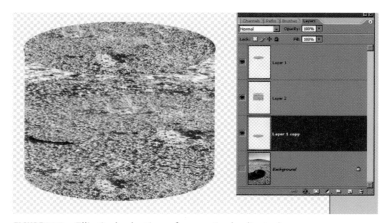

**FIGURE 3.70** Elliptical selection of concrete duplicated.

## Step 3

Add adjustment layers to bring down the density of each image. Use a gradient on the mask of the adjustment layer to create a gradient of the effect (see Figures 3.71 and 3.72).

**FIGURE 3.71**    Gradient applied to Levels adjustment layer.

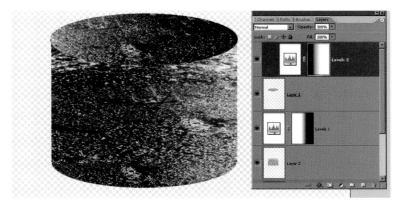

**FIGURE 3.72**    Second Gradient applied to adjustment layer.

## Step 4

Merge all of the concrete layers into a new layer. Remember, hold down the Alt key as you click Merge Layers in the Layers submenu (see Figure 3.73).

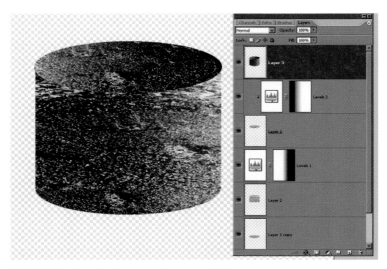

**FIGURE 3.73**    Levels adjustment layer applied.

## Step 5

Place the concrete layer into a layer set titled "Layer Supports" to keep them organized. Continue by applying a mask to blend the pillar with the concrete base, as shown in Figure 3.74.

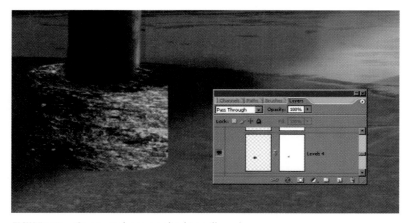

**FIGURE 3.74**    Concrete base applied to pillar.

### Step 6

Apply the support to all of the pillars by duplicating and resizing each one to fit each base, as shown in Figure 3.75.

### Step 7

Since the foreground pillar is over water, create a reflection for it, as shown in Figure 3.76.

**FIGURE 3.76**    Reflection applied to pillar.

**FIGURE 3.75**    Concrete base applied to pillar.

## APPLYING DEPTH OF FIELD

To give the scene a photographic sense of depth you need to apply some depth of field techniques that consist of controlled Gaussian Blurs.

### Step 1

Duplicate the right bridge layer and place it into its own layer set and call it "right bridge blur." Next, apply some Gaussian Blur (Filter > Blur > Gaussian Blur) to give it a slight blur (see Figure 3.77).

**FIGURE 3.77**    Gaussian Blur applied to the right bridge duplicate.

## Step 2

Apply a layer mask and edit it so that the foreground pillar and the front section of the bridge are unaffected by the blur and the background slowly loses depth (see Figure 3.78).

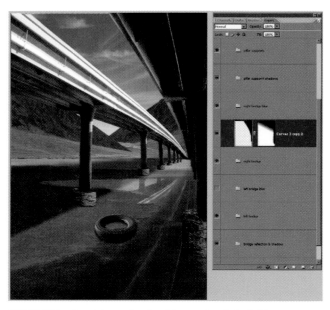

**FIGURE 3.78**    Applying selective blur to the right bridge.

## Step 3

Repeat Step 2 for the left bridge, as shown in Figures 3.79 and 3.80.

**FIGURE 3.79**    Applying Gaussian Blur to the left bridge.

**FIGURE 3.80**    Applying selective blur to the left bridge.

## Step 4

Next, apply a Curves adjustment layer to the background to give it a more dramatic effect (see Figure 3.81).

**FIGURE 3.81**    Applying Curves to background.

## Step 5

ON THE CD
Open Adobe Bridge (File > Browse) and navigate the CD-ROM that comes with this book to the Tutorials/ch 3 over pass and open refinery 001.tif.

## Step 6

Place the refinery behind the landscape layer (see Figure 3.82).

## Step 7

Edit the refinery by adding highlights to the right edges of the architecture. Since it is not a prominent part of the scene, use your dodging tool to brighten up the edges (see Figure 3.83).

## Step 8

It's now time to add the final touches with the nik Color Efex Pro 2.0. Access Color Efex Pro 2.0 (in the Demos folder on the CD-ROM) and select the Classical Soft Focus. You should get something similar to the image shown in Figure 3.84.

**FIGURE 3.82**    Refinery behind the landscape layer.

**FIGURE 3.83**    Editing the edges of the refinery.

## Step 9

Bicolor Brown in combination with the Classical Soft Focus worked very well (see Figure 3.85).

It's complete! Let's move on to learn creative ways to apply effects from scratch.

**FIGURE 3.84**    Classical Soft Focus full view.

**FIGURE 3.85**    Classical Soft Focus with bicolor brown.

**FIGURE 3.86**    Final Result view.

## WHAT YOU HAVE LEARNED

- How to composite photographic imagery
- Practical use of the new HDR Merge
- Smart Objects
- How to use layer sets
- How to use Layer Blending modes
- Free Transform and Distort for localized areas
- Third-party filters to enhance your creations

# 4

# CUSTOM CREATED CONCEPTS

**IN THIS CHAPTER**

- How to use the animated brush engine to custom create smoke effects
- How to use the animated brush engine to custom create debris
- FX tricks to create motion
- Stroke a path with animated brushes
- How to use Quick Mask to define shape

## CUSTOM CREATED METEOR FIELD

We will create the entire meteor scene from scratch with the exception of one image scanned on a flatbed scanner.

Working from photographic content is always less challenging than creating spontaneously because the image speaks to the artist to create in a certain direction. To create from scratch is always much more challenging. Not only do you have to come up with a theme but also you have to render the shapes and textures that will be most convincing to the audience. There are many rendering approaches to consider. This chapter is intended to challenge you to create a meteor field that is convincing to the onlooker. Let's begin.

*Whenever using the Cloud command make sure that the foreground and background color is what you want. Photoshop will use this to create the cloud effect.*

### Step 1

Create two shades of brown and fill the layer with a cloud pattern (Filter > Render > Clouds).

## Step 2

Apply difference clouds (Filter > Render > Difference Clouds) to this layer.

 *Ctrl-F will apply the last filter. This is a handy shortcut.*

## Step 3

Hit Ctrl-F to apply the last filter three separate times. The goal is to gain an aggressive-looking texture (see Figure 4.1).

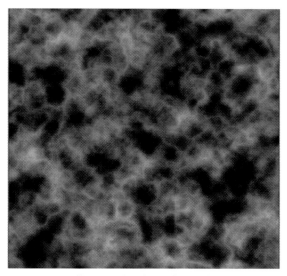

**FIGURE 4.1**    Difference clouds applied a third time.

## Step 4

Access your Channels palette (Windows > Channels) and inspect the black-and-white images to determine which one has the most contrast. We will use this to create a displacement map. The highlight will display height and the shadows will display depth. We will achieve this with the use of the Lighting Effects command. In this example the Red Channel gives you the most contrast (see Figure 4.2).

 *The Lighting Effects Panel will use your channels and alpha channels to produce texture.*

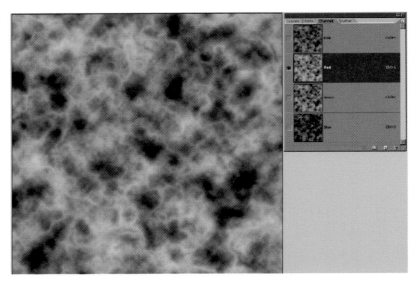

**FIGURE 4.2**    View of the red channel.

## Step 5

First, duplicate your textured layer (Figure 4.3) and then access the Lighting Effects panel (Filter > Render > Lighting Effects). Apply the light source so that the light starts from the upper left and falls off in the lower right. Make sure that the red channel is selected in the Texture Channel box. The tonal information will produce the textured effect we are looking for. Now click OK.

Take a look at the rendered texture file. This will serve as the basis of our meteor texture (see Figure 4.4).

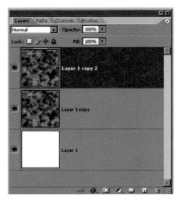

**FIGURE 4.3**    Duplicating the texture layer.

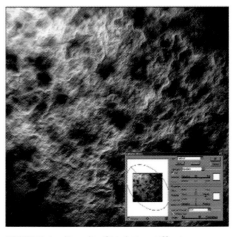

**FIGURE 4.4**    Result of Lighting Effects.

## Step 6

Now let's give the meteor some craters. Access Liquefy (Filter > Liquefy) and use the tool set to create a series of craters (Figure 4.5). When you are done click OK and continue.

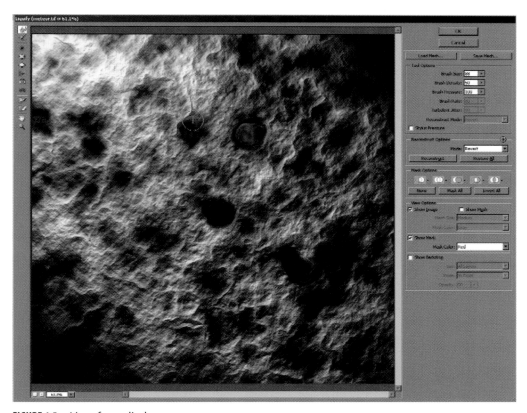

**FIGURE 4.5**    Liquefy applied.

## Step 7

You don't have to create craters over the entire pattern because you will use just a small part of this image. Use your Lasso tool to create a rough outline of the first meteor. Hit Ctrl-J to apply what's in the section to its own layer (see Figure 4.6).

Follow Step 7 to create more meteors on their own layers, as shown in Figure 4.7.

**FIGURE 4.6**    Meteor created.

**FIGURE 4.7**    New Meteors created.

## Step 8

Right-click on each layer and select Group into New Smart Layer to make them Smart Objects. Remember, resizing Smart Objects has no effect on resolution. Resize them so that the ones that you want to give the illusion of distance will be smaller and the ones that are coming forward will be larger (see Figure 4.8).

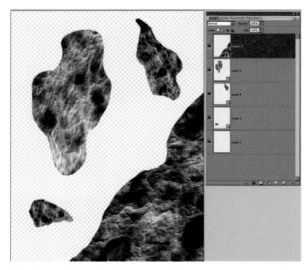

**FIGURE 4.8**    Smart Objects applied.

When completed, select all of the layers by Ctrl-clicking on each of the meteor layers and placing them into their own layer set. Call it "meteors" to be organized (see Figure 4.9).

## Step 9

From the CD-ROM access `Tutorials/ch 4 meteor/stone-1.tif`. The initial rock was scanned using an HP 6300 flatbed scanner. Several photos were scanned at a resolution of 1200 ppi (pixels per inch).

*Remember that the better your resolution is when you scan, the more effective Photoshop can be when you use selections.*

If you choose to scan your own stones, then use Quick Mask to select the rock's background to isolate it, as shown in Figure 4.10. The clear area is the selected object and the areas in red are masked out.

**FIGURE 4.9**    Result of layer changes.

**FIGURE 4.10**    Quick Mask inversed.

Now enter back into the Normal Selection mode (Q) to view the result and drag the stone into the meteor image (see Figure 4.11).

## Step 10

Use Perspective (Edit > Transform > Perspective) to simulate the stone extending into the foreground. This will become the supersized meteor that will be composed underneath the rest (see Figure 4.12).

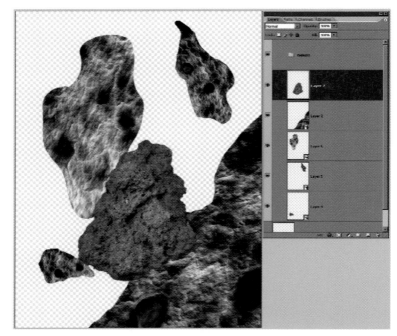

**FIGURE 4.11**     Stone dragged into meteor file.

**FIGURE 4.12**     Result of Perspective in Step 10.

## Step 11

Now give the stone a texture with more of a surface relief to it. Access the Lighting Effects panel (Filter > Render > Lighting Effects) and apply the same lighting used for the initial meteor. Select the Red channel for your texture and click OK (see Figures 4.13 and 4.14).

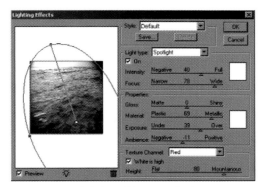

**FIGURE 4.13**    Lighting Effects applied.

**FIGURE 4.14**    Result of Lighting Effects.

## Step 12

Duplicate this layer and set the blend mode to Multiply. Reduce its opacity to around 75%. This is a good time to place these layers into their own layer set called "surface" (see Figure 4.15).

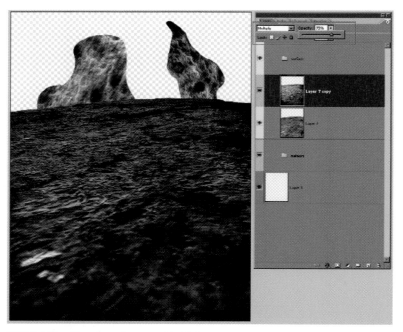

**FIGURE 4.15**    Blend mode set to Multiply.

## Step 13

Duplicate this layer again and set the blend mode to Color Burn. Give it a layer mask filled with black and edit it by painting with white to create the effect of deep crevasses in the rock, as shown in Figure 4.16.

## Step 14

Next, place the surface layer set below the meteor layer set to allow the others to float above it. Start with the larger meteor in the foreground and duplicate it (Ctrl-J). Right click on this layer and choose Rasterize Layer. A Smart Objects layer must be rasterized to edit anything on the image.

Apply some Motion Blur to the layer (Filter > Blur > Motion Blur), as shown in Figure 4.17.

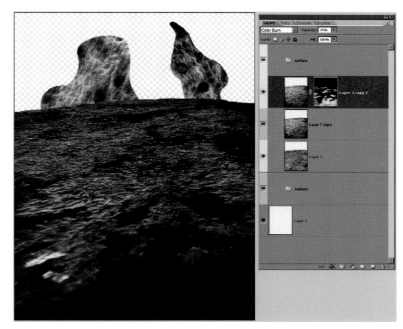

**FIGURE 4.16**    Result of editing the mask in Step 13.

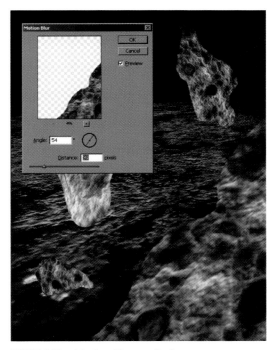

**FIGURE 4.17**    Motion Blur applied.

### Step 15

Create two new adjustment layers: Curves and Levels. Adjust the tonal information so that the deeper tones will dominate the image. Isolate these adjustments to the foreground meteor layer by holding down the Alt key and clicking between the meteor layer and the adjustment layer.

Now edit the masks to allow the peaks of the meteor to become more highlighted. The light source will come from the rear. We will add it later (see Figure 4.18).

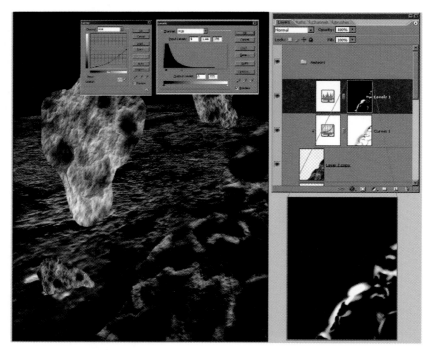

**FIGURE 4.18**    Final result of Step 15.

### Step 16

Select the meteor layer that rests in the top-left corner. We will add some pixel effects, so don't forget to rasterize it. Select the shape and apply Liquefy (Filters > Liquefy) to give it additional crater detail, as shown in Figure 4.19).

### Step 17

Apply the Curves and Levels adjustment layers as you did in Step 15. Be creative and don't be afraid to experiment with other tonal adjustments (see Figure 4.20).

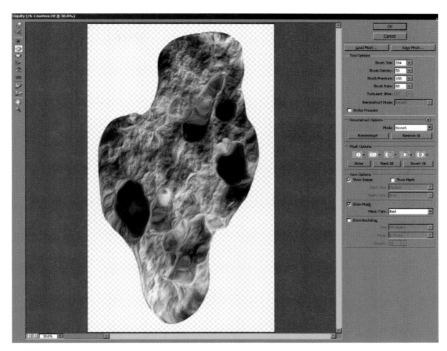

**FIGURE 4.19**    Liquefy applied.

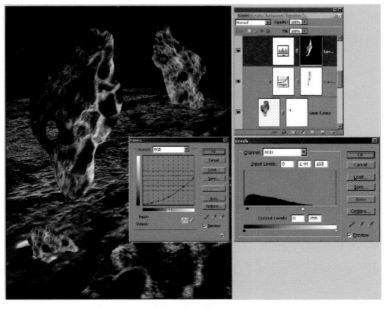

**FIGURE 4.20**    View of Curves and Levels adjustments.

### Step 18

Apply the Curves and Levels adjustment layer to the meteor layer in the top right (see Figure 4.21).

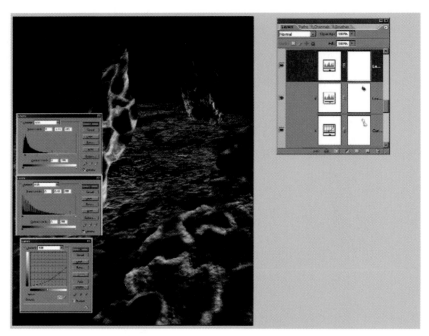

**FIGURE 4.21** Final result of Step 18.

## ADDING THE LIGHT SOURCE

We have added lighting details and now it's time to create the source from which the light emanates. So, let's create a star in the background.

### Step 1

Start by creating a new layer and filling it with medium gray (Edit > Fill > Fill with 50% Gray).

### Step 2

Apply Lens Flare to the medium gray layer and change the blend mode to Hard Light.

## Step 3

Free Transform (Edit > Free Transform) the Lens Flare and duplicate it. Place one above the meteors layer set and the other below the "surface" layer set (see Figure 4.22).

**FIGURE 4.22**    Lens Flare transformed.

## Step 4

Apply a levels adjustment layer to the planetoid and reduce its density. Then apply a gradient from black to white from the top to the bottom of the mask to allow the effect to become isolated to the foreground, as shown in Figure 4.23.

## Step 5

Create a new layer and fill it with white. This will become the gaseous atmosphere around the planetoid. Use your eraser tool to shape the white color to the shape of the planetoid. Next apply some Gaussian Blur (Filter > Blur > Gaussian Blur), as shown in Figure 4.24.

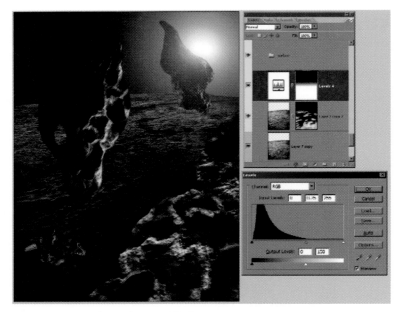

**FIGURE 4.23** Levels gradient applied.

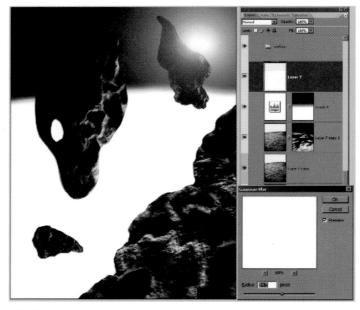

**FIGURE 4.24** Create white shape.

## Step 6

Apply a Gradient Mask to the white shape layer to allow the effects to reside in the background of the planetoid, and not in the front. This will give the scene a little more depth (see Figure 4.25).

**FIGURE 4.25**    Apply Gradient Mask.

## Step 7

Change the color of the star to a warmer light source like yellow using Hue/Saturation (Ctrl-U), as shown in Figure 4.26.

## Step 8

It's a good idea to change the color of the gas overlay to match the color source of the star, so we duplicate its layer and fill it with yellow. Make sure the Lock Transparency button is selected otherwise the entire layer will be filled with yellow (see Figure 4.27).

**FIGURE 4.26**    Change the color of the star.

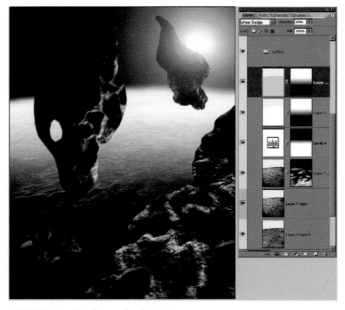

**FIGURE 4.27**    Gas layer duplicated.

## ADJUSTING THE LIGHT SOURCE

Next, we will add some mood to the scene with the introduction of volumetric light rays. These light rays will extend from the light source toward the viewer. This will further assist the composition by leading the viewer's eye into and around the scene.

### Step 1

Access File > Automate > nik 2.0 Selective to get the Selective panel and select the Fog Filter. Experiment with your own settings. Click OK when you're done then click Apply on the 2.0 Selective panel for the effect. By default, the mask is black, so fill it with white so that you can see the effect over the entire scene.

### Step 2

The filter merges everything into one layer to apply its effects. You want to apply the fog to selected areas of the image to simulate light streaks. So create a shape similar to Figure 4.28 where the shadow starts from the rear meteor and extends toward the foreground. Keep in mind that as shapes come forward they become larger and as they recede they become smaller. Fill the selection with black on the mask.

**FIGURE 4.28**    Mask of edited gas layer.

## Step 3

The results from Step 2 are too harsh. Let's add some subtlety. Increase the brightness of the mask so that you will get the effect of different densities of fog in the background as well as in the foreground, as shown in Figure 4.29.

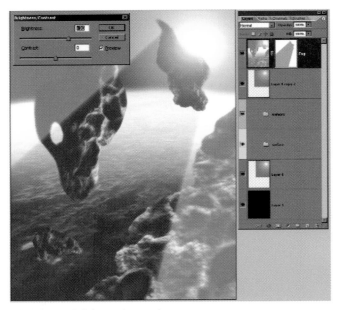

**FIGURE 4.29**    Brighten the mask.

## Step 4

Continue to edit the mask to add similar effects to the other meteors. The use of the paintbrush tool is advantageous here. Figure 4.30 shows the progression.

## Step 5

Duplicate this layer and change the blend mode to Vivid Light, as shown in Figure 4.31.

## Step 6

Fill its mask with black to block out its effect. Use your paintbrush tool to apply the effect to the surface areas of the two meteors in the foreground only. This gives additional depth to the scene (see Figure 4.32).

**FIGURE 4.30**    More light streaks added.

**FIGURE 4.31**    Duplicate the layer.

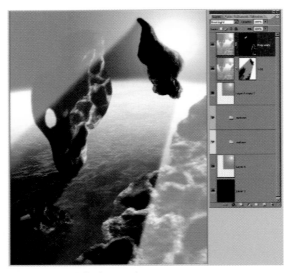

**FIGURE 4.32** Edit the mask.

## Step 7

Now we will add some dust-like debris. Add two new layers and fill them with 50% gray (Edit > Fill > Fill with 50% gray) and add noise (Filter > Noise > Add Noise).

Change the blend modes on both to Hard Light so that all you see is the noise pattern, which will look like microscopic debris (see Figure 4.33).

**FIGURE 4.33** Add debris.

Adjust the opacity of the layers to achieve a mood that appeals to you. Figure 4.34 shows the completed image.

**FIGURE 4.34**    Final image.

## CUSTOM CREATED TORNADO

In this section you will use a custom-animated brush that you will create from scratch to create most of the tornado effects. Once you understand the brush palette, what you can create is limited only to your imagination. In *Photoshop CS Trickery and FX* you were introduced to the animated engine to create smoke. Now you will use the tool more extensively to create several brushes to produce the tornado scene. Let's begin.

### Step 1

Open a new layer that is 2 × 2 inches and a resolution of 200 ppi. You will use this new file as your scratch pad to create your custom brushes. Make sure that your paintbrush tool is selected. Create a new layer and paint a smoke shape in a circular pattern on this layer (see Figures 4.35 and 4.36).

### Step 2

Create a new brush from this shape (Edit > Define New Brush Preset). Call it what you like, for example, "Smoke 001."

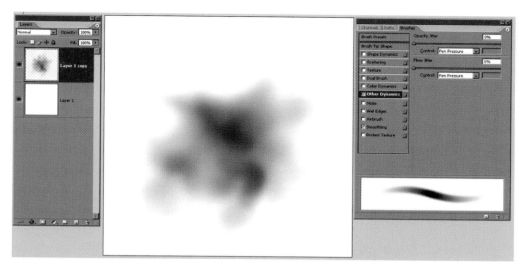

**FIGURE 4.35**    Create a new layer and initial brush pattern.

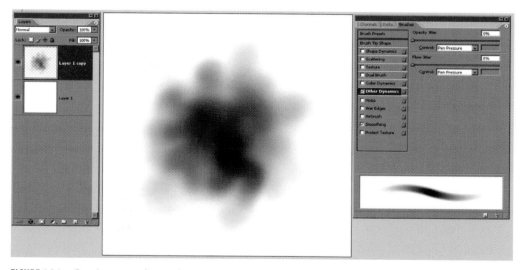

**FIGURE 4.36**    Continue to edit smoke pattern.

## Step 3

Take a look at your Brush Preset options (Windows > Brushes). This gives you a visual of what the stroke will look like when it's applied to the canvas. Let's make some changes (see Figure 4.37).

### Step 4

Click the Shape Dynamics box to view options for changing the size of the brush over the length of the stroke. Adjust them to get something like that shown in Figure 4.38 and do the same for "Scattering." Remember to experiment. These are only suggestions.

*The Shape Dynamics is great for adding a sense of animation to your brush shapes.*

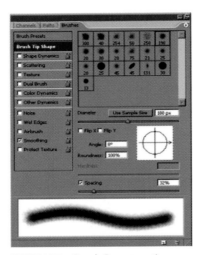

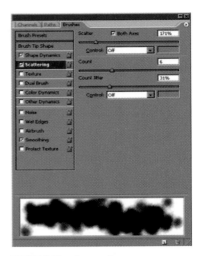

**FIGURE 4.37**   Brush Preset options.        **FIGURE 4.38**   Scattering.

## Step 5

The Color Dynamics will blend the foreground and background colors as you paint over time. Use of this option is very helpful for smoke-like atmospheres. Since the colors that you will be working with are shades of gray, you only need to adjust the "foreground/background" jitter and "brightness" jitter. Take note that there is no visual update for this. You will have to paint on the canvas to view the results.

## Step 6

Next, tell the program to use the WACOM pen's pressure to apply opacity.

If you don't have a WACOM pen you can still achieve these effects by manually adjusting the opacity slider on the options bar (see Figure 4.39).

## Step 7

After you create the new dynamics for the brush you will need to save it as a new brush or you will lose it when you close Photoshop. Access the submenu and click New Brush Preset.

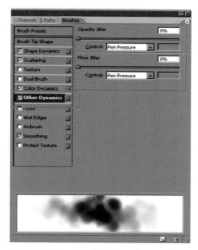

**FIGURE 4.39**    Apply Other Dynamics.

## Step 8

Delete the original brush shape and paint with the new one in a circular pattern using the new Tornado Smoke 001 brush as shown in Figure 4.40.

Now define this shape as a New Brush Preset and call it "Tornado Brush2." Give it the same dynamics as the Tornado Smoke Brush 001.

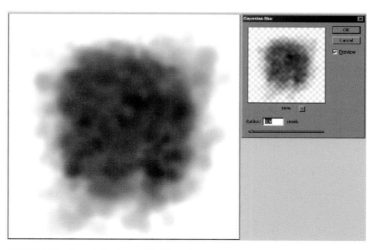

**FIGURE 4.40**    Brush test used in Step 7.

## Step 9

Delete the original brush shape on the layer and paint with the new Tornado Brush 2 in a circular pattern as shown in Figure 4.41.

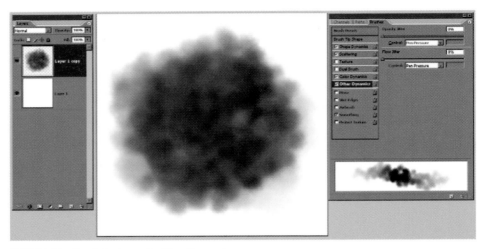

**FIGURE 4.41**  Brush test used in Step 9.

Give this the same dynamics as the Tornado Brush 2 but this time select the Dual Brush dialog box and select the Tornado Smoke Brush 001. Now the brush places two different brush dynamics into one. Adjust your scattering to become a little tighter to give you more control (see Figure 4.42). Save this as a new brush and call it "Tornado Smoke Brush 003."

**FIGURE 4.42**  New brush scattering adjusted.

## STARTING THE TORNADO

Now that all of the brushes are defined let's develop the funnel of the tornado.

### Step 1

Create a new file that is 10 × 12 inches at 300 ppi. Make sure that the Paintbrush is selected and paint a smoke pattern over the entire image, as shown in Figure 4.43.

*There are some custom brushes on the CD-ROM in the* Tutorials/Custom Brushes *folder that you can use instead of creating your own. Load* Tornado Brushes.abr, *if you prefer to use our pre-made brushes.*

### Step 2

Change the brush blend mode of the brush to Multiply and paint a series of vertical darkened cloud streaks as shown in Figure 4.44.

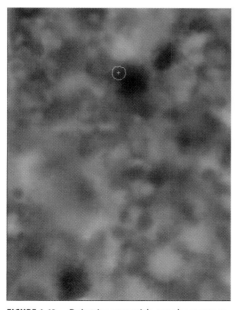

**FIGURE 4.43**    Paint image with smoke pattern.

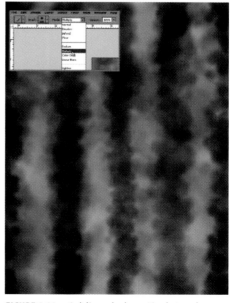

**FIGURE 4.44**    Adding dark vertical streaks.

### Step 3

Apply the twirl filter (Filter > Distort > Twirl) to layer to start the funnel shape.

### Step 4

In Tutorials/ch 4 tornado on the CD-ROM open the road & sky.tif image and drag it into your tornado file. Resize the image to fit the entire screen. Place this image into a layer set called "road and sky" underneath the tornado layer.

Use the transform command (Ctrl-T) to truncate and offset the beginnings of the tornado shape into the sky portion of your image. Use Figure 4.45 as a guide.

**FIGURE 4.45**    Twirl filter & Transform applied.

### Step 5

Create a new layer. On this layer reduce the size of your brush using your bracket key ( [ ) and paint smaller cloud patterns while following the shapes of the twirl. Place both of these layers into a new layer set called "Tornado" (see Figure 4.46).

### Step 6

Repeat Step 5 and change the blend modes from Multiply to Lighten to build contour to the shape, as shown in Figure 4.47.

**FIGURE 4.46**    Twirl pattern edited.

**FIGURE 4.47**    Final twirl contour.

### Step 7

Next, add a sense of wind effects. Duplicate the current layer (Ctrl-J) to apply the next effect to it. Use the Elliptical selection tool to outline the cloud shape. Next, add a Radial Blur with a slight zoom. Figure 4.48 shows the result of the Radial Blur.

Duplicate this layer and add some more cloud detail as you did in Step 5. If necessary, add layer masks to assist you in shaping your image.

**FIGURE 4.48**    Result of the Radial Blur.

## ADDING THE TAIL TO THE TORNADO

You will now add the custom paintbrush effect to a defined path using the Pen tool. This shape will be edited to define the shape and feel of a tornado tail.

### Step 1

Select the Pen tool on the Tools bar and apply a shape that starts from the center of the twirl and ends near the midsection of the road.

### Step 2

Select the Paintbrush again. You should still be using the last brush that you used to created the cloud swirl. You can use this one for the tail as well. Place your brush along the path near the center of the swirl. Adjust the size of the mouse to match the size that you would like the tail to be using the bracket keys, [ and ] on the keyboard (see Figure 4.49).

**FIGURE 4.49**    Adjust the size of the mouse.

Take a look at the Path palette (Windows > Path) and locate a series of icons in the lower section. Click the second icon from the left to stroke the path with the brush dynamics.

Figure 4.50 shows the result of the stroke that you have just applied. You can experiment using some of the other custom brushes. In fact, apply a variety of the custom brushes on top of each other and view how they blend with one another.

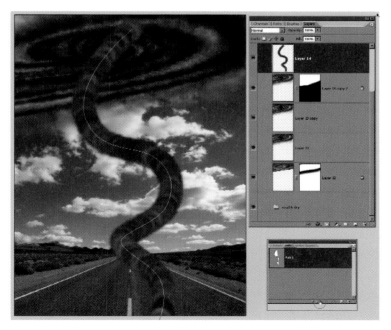

**FIGURE 4.50**    Result of the outline.

### Step 3

Use the Perspective tool (Edit > Transform > Perspective), as shown in Figure 4.51.

**FIGURE 4.51**    Apply Perspective.

### Step 4

Next, use the Shear command (Filter > Distort > Shear) to add more flow to the tail (see Figure 4.52).

### Step 5

Apply a layer mask to the tail to shape it. Hit the \ key to change the mask to a Quick Mask view and edit the shape using the Paintbrush.

*Insisting on absolute control in the early stages can stagnate the creative process and can hamper your seeing alternative approaches. Work fairly loose in the beginning and later allow alternative possibilities to complete your final vision.*

Remember, to add to the red mask you paint with black and to subtract from the mask you paint with white. Figure 4.53 shows the finished result. Hit \ again to return

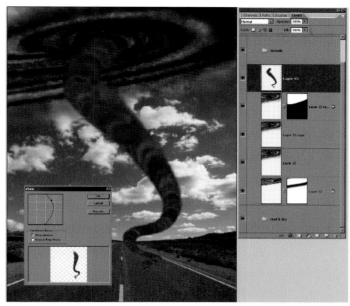

**FIGURE 4.52**    Apply Shear.

**FIGURE 4.53**    Final result of Step 5.

to the normal view. At this stage the shape is a basic "S" curve. Nature however, provides quite a number of variations for tornados. Some have funnels that are very linear and thin, and others have funnels that are fat and short. Try not to place too much effort in getting the perfect shape because later you are going to transform it into a modified curve. Often we spend too much time trying to control the creative process because we are too attached to our creative technique. For now, simply use the mask to paint in the basic shape of your choice.

### Step 6

Moving forward, duplicate the tail layer and add some noise. This is necessary to assist Step 7.

### Step 7

Apply Motions Blur (Filter > Blur > Motion Blur) and match the angle shown in Figure 4.54. As you can see, the noise from Step 6 helped to give the blur some textural grooves.

**FIGURE 4.54**    Apply Motion Blur.

### Step 8

Create a new layer and apply some dust effects around the tail with the smoke brushes (see Figure 4.55).

**FIGURE 4.55**    Apply dust.

### Step 9

Create another layer and apply the same effects to the foreground of the swirl. Additionally, add some Motion Blur to simulate the rotating motion (see Figure 4.56).

### Step 10

Select another custom brush and on another layer apply cloud effects on the background of the tornado. Use a small brush size to achieve this since anything in the background will appear smaller. Now, just as you did in Step 9, apply Motion Blur to accentuate the theme of movement (see Figure 4.57).

### Step 11

Duplicate this layer twice and change the blend mode to Darken to obtain a deeper tonality that will further portray a greater sense of depth (see Figure 4.58).

Select all three of the layers and merge them, as shown in Figure 4.59.

### Step 12

Access the CD-ROM and open Cloud 01.tif from the Tutorials/ch 4 tornado folder.

ON THE CD

**FIGURE 4.56** Apply dust to swirl.

**FIGURE 4.57** Apply Motion Blur.

**FIGURE 4.59**    Result of merging in Step 12.

**FIGURE 4.58**    Duplicate layers.

## Step 13

Place this image into the road and sky layer group above the road and sky image.

## Step 14

Hit Ctrl-T to resize your clouds a bit larger (see Figure 4.60).

**FIGURE 4.60**    Cloud image resized.

**Step 15**

Turn off the Tornado layer set so that you will have fewer distractions for the next steps. Apply the clouds only above the horizon on the mountain range. Use Quick Mask to achieve this (see Figure 4.61).

**FIGURE 4.61**    Quick Mask applied.

When completed, apply this as a layer mask to the cloud image (see Figure 4.62).

**Step 16**

Turn on the Tornado layer set to view the results then duplicate the cloud layer and add noise (see Figure 4.63).

**FIGURE 4.62**    Layer Mask applied.

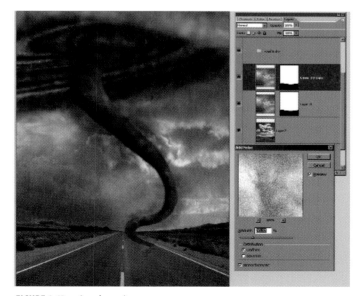

**FIGURE 4.63**    Apply noise.

## Step 17

Next, add some Motion Blur (see Figure 4.64).

## Step 18

Add a Gradient Mask to the motion blur to allow the effects to become isolated to the foreground of the image, as shown in Figure 4.65.

**FIGURE 4.64**    Apply Motion Blur.

**FIGURE 4.65**    Apply a Gradient Mask.

## ADDING GROUND EFFECTS

When the tail of the tornado touches the ground it whips up an aggressive display of dust twirling around the tip of the tail. You will use some of the elements that you have already created to achieve this.

### Step 1

Select one of the spiral effects in the Tornado layer set and duplicate it. Place it on top, and then rotate it and place it at the base of the tail (see Figure 4.66).

**FIGURE 4.66**    Rotate spiral effect layer.

### Step 2

Place an oval selection on it and apply a Zoom Radial Blur (see Figure 4.67).

### Step 3

Use Distort (Edit > Transform > Distort) to force the fringed tips upward (see Figure 4.68). Figure 4.69 shows the end results.

The ground effects are complete, so let's add some debris to our scene.

**FIGURE 4.67** Apply a Zoom Blur.

**FIGURE 4.68** Apply Distort.

**FIGURE 4.69** Apply Mask to Zoom Blur.

## ADDING DEBRIS

You will create another custom brush for the debris. This will assist you with making a selection to create the debris from the road image.

### Step 1

Create the basic shape of your debris and define it as a brush preset with scattering and sizing options turned on (see Figure 4.70).

**FIGURE 4.70**    Debris effect defined.

### Step 2

Turn off all of the layers except the road and sky layer and create a new layer above it. Paint with black on the road location. Ctrl-click on this layer to create a selection of the brush pattern you have created (see Figure 4.71).

### Step 3

Select the road layer and hit Ctrl-C and Ctrl-V to copy and paste its information into a new layer (see Figure 4.72).

### Step 4

Turn on the other layers and place the new debris layer into its own layer set and title it "foreground debris" (see Figure 4.73).

**FIGURE 4.71**   Debris applied.

**FIGURE 4.72**   Copy and paste debris.

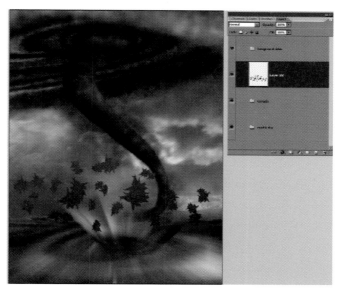

**FIGURE 4.73**    Foreground debris layer set.

## Step 5

Flip this layer vertically (Edit > Transform > Flip 90 Degrees CW) and add Motion Blur (Figure 4.74) and Shear to give the illusion that the debris is rotating around the tornado. Shear only works vertically. This is why it was necessary to flip the debris.

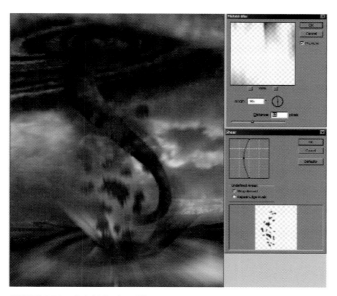

**FIGURE 4.74**    Add Motion Blur.

## Step 6

Use Distort to create depth from the background to foreground, as shown in Figure 4.75.

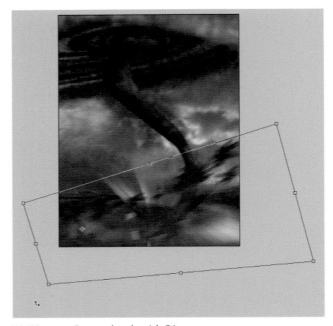

**FIGURE 4.75** Create depth with Distort.

## Step 7

Double click on the right empty portion of the layer to bring up the layer effects dialog box and add Bevel and Emboss. Experiment with these settings to achieve a 3D effect. When you are finished, increase the contrast using levels (see Figures 4.76 and 4.77).

## Step 8

Adjust the scattering on the Debris brush so that it is tighter and reduce the brush size for the background debris. Paint some debris vertically down the center to give the image a slightly circular shape

When you are done give it a vertical motion blur, as shown in Figure 4.78.

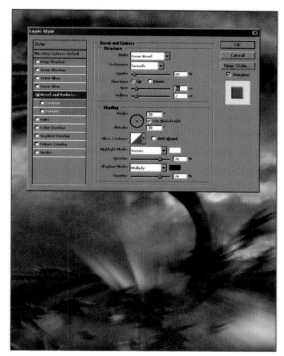

**FIGURE 4.76**    Add Bevel and Emboss.

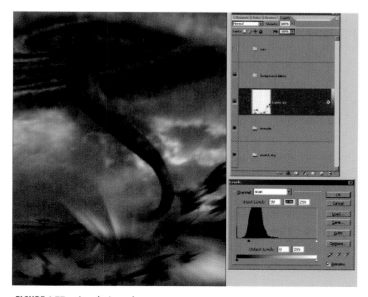

**FIGURE 4.77**    Apply Levels.

**FIGURE 4.78**    Add Motion Blur.

### Step 9

Use Transform (Ctrl-T) to reposition the debris horizontally along the base of the tail (see Figure 4.79).

Duplicate the layer, resize the debris, and place them into the scene. This will not only add more debris but also will offset it. Use layer masking to blend them with the rest of the scenes so that they are not too visually dominating (see Figure 4.80).

### Step 10

Add a little more form to the funnel of the tornado. Select the Smudge tool and under Mode, choose lighten on the options bar.

### Step 11

Select one of the texture brushes and turn off all of the dynamics so that you can apply Linear Smudge stroke. Smudge the lighter tone into the darker ones to accentuate motion and texture (see Figure 4.81).

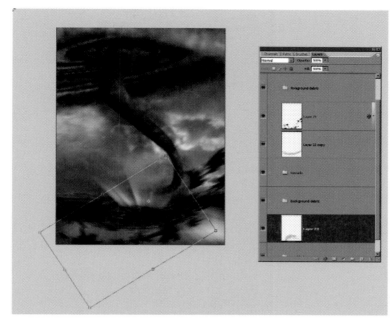

**FIGURE 4.79**   Transform the background debris.

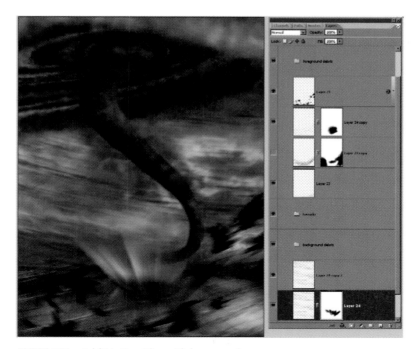

**FIGURE 4.80**   Add Motion Blur with layer mask.

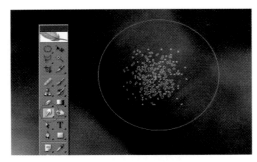

**FIGURE 4.81**    Apply the Smudge tool.

## Step 12

Select several portions of the funnel and apply more Motion Blur but apply the angle according to the direction of the funnel, as shown in Figure 4.82.

## Step 13

Let's add an explosive effect to the base of the funnel. Select the Shape tool and make an oval horizontal ellipse.

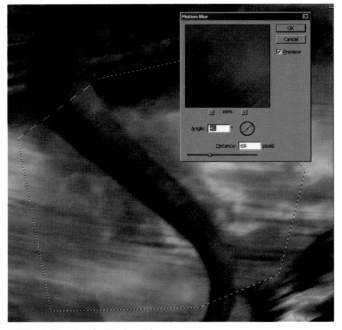

**FIGURE 4.82**    Apply Motion Blur.

## Step 14

Now, we will add some color and contrast effects to make the final image more dynamic. Apply a Hue/Saturation adjustment layer and hit Colorize. In this example the settings give the image a sepia effect. Additionally, the mask is edited to allow the original color of the sky to show through the background (see Figure 4.83).

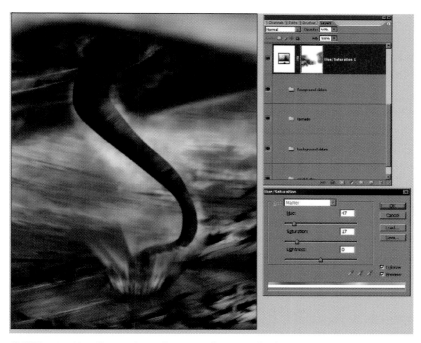

**FIGURE 4.83**   Hue/Saturation adjustment layer applied.

## Step 15

Remember when we talked about being open to other possibilities? This where we are going to apply another look to the funnel. Now that we have all of the detail and color alterations established for the tail, we will apply the Perspective tool (Edit > Transform > Perspective) and narrow the base of the funnel, as shown in Figure 4.84.

## Step 16

Use your tornado brushes to apply more clouds to the upper portion of the tornado and apply some Radial Blur to give them a sense of motion (see Figure 4.85).

**FIGURE 4.84**    Apply Perspective to the funnel.

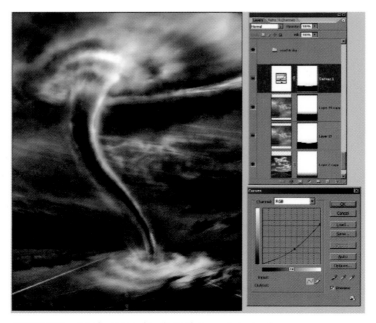

**FIGURE 4.85**    Apply more clouds to the upper tornado.

## Step 17

For the final touches open the nik Color Efex Pro 2.0 Selective and choose Bicolor Warm.

Apply the effects as shown in Figure 4.86.

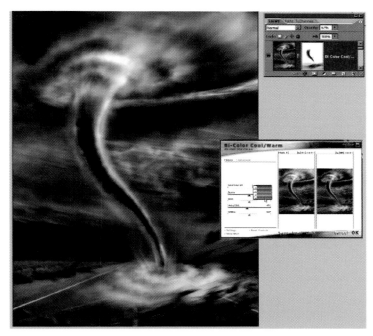

**FIGURE 4.86**    Nik Color Efex Pro 2.0 Bicolor Warm.

## Step 18

When done, change the layer's opacity to 62% and edit the mask with the Paintbrush to bring in the original whites of the lower dust cloud below the tail.

Figure 4.87 shows the completed image. It's okay if yours looks slightly different. The steps provided here are only suggestions. Feel free to elaborate on them.

**FIGURE 4.87**  The final tornado result.

## WHAT YOU HAVE LEARNED

- How to utilize the animated brush engine to custom create smoke and debris
- FX tricks to create motion
- Stroke a path with animated brushes
- How to use Quick Mask to define shape

# INTEGRATING 3D OBJECTS

## IN THIS CHAPTER

- How to use the animated brush engine to custom create explosion effects
- How to use nik Color Efex Pro 2.0 to assist in creating explosion effects
- FX tricks to create motion
- How to apply the Warp tool
- How to use photographic images to create explosive effects

## CREATING THE INITIAL LANDSCAPE

In this chapter we will use digital RAW images created with the Canon 10 D. All of the images were shot along Highway 1 and the Carmel, California coastline. The lighting was overcast, which made it perfect for scenic photographs. The diffused lighting allowed all of the details to show through wonderfully.

You will use several of these images to create a composited landscape as the backdrop of the 3D android crouched in the river underneath the bridge. The surrounding landscape will be reflected in the body of the droid that has already been created for you in LightWave 8.0.

In addition you will create the reflections in the riverbed to make the scene more convincing.

### Step 1

ON THE CD

Go to the Tutorials/ch 5 landscape folder on the CD-ROM and open pfiefer beach river.crw, Coastal Bridge.crw, and pfiefer beach.tif in Photoshop (see Figures 5.1 through 5.3).

**FIGURE 5.1**    pfiefer beach river.crw.

**FIGURE 5.3**    pfiefer beach.tif.

**FIGURE 5.2**    Coastal Bridge.crw.

## Step 2

Open the files in the Adobe Raw interface and apply the settings that work best for you. The example here is only a suggested starting point. Save the settings that you apply to the first image and apply it to the other two for consistency. Commit your settings and let's move on (see Figure 5.4).

## Step 3

Enlarge the image using Free Transform (Ctrl-T) to allow the river to dominate the lower third section of the composition (see Figure 5.5).

**FIGURE 5.4**   Adobe Raw interface.

**FIGURE 5.5**   Image enlarged.

## Step 4

Duplicate this layer and change the blend mode to Multiply. This will add some richness to the overall scene. Add a layer mask filled with black by Alt-clicking on the Layer Mask icon and edit it using your Paintbrush so that the Multiply effect is isolated to the river, as shown in Figure 5.6.

**FIGURE 5.6**    Apply Mask and Multiply blend mode.

## Step 5

Place the Pfiefer Beach image into this file and apply it as a Smart Object, as shown in Figure 5.7.

**FIGURE 5.7**    Smart Object applied.

You have applied a Smart Object so that the detail and quality is maintained as you adjust the size of the image. If it is reduced and enlarged again with Free Transform the image quality is maintained to the way it was originally as shown in Figures 5.8 and 5.9.

**FIGURE 5.8**    Smart Object reduced.

**FIGURE 5.9**    Smart Object enlarged.

For now, reduce the image so that the stone sits in the lower-right corner of the screen. Apply a mask so that it integrates with the existing sand (see Figures 5.10 and 5.11).

**FIGURE 5.11**    Apply Mask to Smart Object.

**FIGURE 5.10**    Compose Smart Object.

## Step 6

Apply a Curves Adjustment layer to increase the contrast a bit to match the overall contrast of the scene, as shown in Figure 5.12.

## Step 7

ON THE CD

Access the Tutorials/ch 5 landscape folder on the CD-ROM and open Carmel fence.tif. Place the fence image above the river. After committing it as a Smart Object, resize and position the fence above the grassy bank on the lower left, as shown in Figure 5.13.

## Step 8

Apply a layer mask to integrate the fence into the river scene. Use a soft-edge paintbrush to achieve this. Remember, if you hit the \ key the black portions of the mask will show up as red. This makes it easier for you to see where you are working in relation to the image (see Figures 5.14 and 5.15).

**FIGURE 5.12**    Apply Curves adjustment.

**FIGURE 5.13**    Smart Object applied.

**FIGURE 5.15**    Layer view of Mask.

**FIGURE 5.14**    Apply Mask to the fence.

## Step 9

Make contrast changes to the transformed fence by linking a Curves adjustment layer as you did to the stone image (see Figure 5.16).

**FIGURE 5.16**    Contrast alterations to stone.

### Step 10

Place the bridge image you opened in Step 1 on top of the river and fence layers and place all of them into their own layer set titled "bridge." Don't forget to designate it as a Smart Object (see Figure 5.17).

### Step 11

Resize the bridge as shown in Figure 5.18 for a more dynamic appeal.

**FIGURE 5.18**    Bridge resized.

**FIGURE 5.17**    Bridge placed into file.

### Step 12

Apply a layer mask and use a soft-edge paintbrush to edit the mask so that the areas underneath the arch allow the detail from the river scene to come through (see Figure 5.19).

### Step 13

Now that the bridge is over the water you will need to add its reflection. Duplicate the bridge layer (Ctrl-J) and invert the layer vertically (Edit > Transform > Flip Vertical) and position it so that the tip of the arch is in the river. Associate a black filled layer mask and paint with white to reveal the reflection in the river. Use Figure 5.20 as a guide.

**FIGURE 5.19**    Bridge layer is masked.

**FIGURE 5.20**    Reflection of bridge in the water.

## Step 14

The color balance of the bridge doesn't quite match up to the rest of the scene. It needs to take on the greenish ambient light that is being bounced from the foliage. So, apply Color Balance adjustment layers to the bridge only (see Figure 5.21).

**FIGURE 5.21**   Apply Color Balance to the bridge.

## Step 15

The overall scene is tonally a little flat, so we will improve it with the use of Curves, as shown in Figure 5.22.

## Step 16

ON THE CD

Go to the `Tutorials/ch 5 landscape` folder on the CD-ROM and open the `spider droid final.tif` image. Place it into its own layer set called "spider droid" (see Figure 5.23).

## Step 17

Apply a layer mask and edit out the tips of the feet so that the droid appears to be submerged in the water (see Figure 5.24).

**FIGURE 5.22**    Apply Curves to the bridge.

**FIGURE 5.23**    Apply spider droid image.

### Step 18

Duplicate the spider droid layer and flip it vertically to use as the reflection. Apply the same technique as you did in Step 13 (see Figure 5.25).

**FIGURE 5.24** Apply Mask to the spider droid image.

**FIGURE 5.25** Flip the spider droid image.

### Step 19

Duplicate the inversed spider droid layer to apply the reflection of the rear leg in the back section of the river. Make sure that you align the two correctly. Apply the same mask technique as you did in Step 13 (see Figure 5.26).

### Step 20

Fill the mask with black and allow only the rear leg image to manifest itself in the water, as shown in Figure 5.27. Although you can select a portion of the legs and cut and paste them into their proper location, it is advantageous to have the complete image and use masks to allow only what you choose to show through. If you should ever want to go back to improve upon your image or include other parts of it the entire image will still be at your command.

### Step 21

Duplicate the inversed spider droid layer again and fill it will black (Edit > Fill > Fill with Black). Make sure the Preserve Transparent Pixels box is selected so that the shape of the droid is filled with black and not the entire layer (see Figure 5.28).

**FIGURE 5.26**    Flip the spider droid image duplicated.

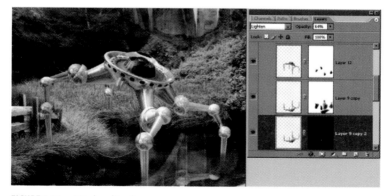

**FIGURE 5.27**    Mask edited.

When complete, reduce the transparency of the layer and set its blend mode to Multiply (see Figure 5.29).

Now give this a mask to restrict the shadow to the grassy region (see Figure 5.30).

**FIGURE 5.28** Fill spider droid with black.

**FIGURE 5.29** Spider droid shadow is reduced in opacity.

**FIGURE 5.30** Mask applied to shadow.

## CREATING LASER EFFECT

The spider droid is emitting a particle beam from its snout. When the beam causes a glow as it hits the water, steam lifts from the heated area.

### Step 1

So let's start by creating the Flare Effect. Apply Lens Flare to a new layer filled with 50% gray (see Figures 5.31 and 5.32).

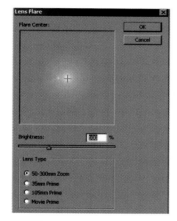

**FIGURE 5.31**  Lens Flare dialog box.

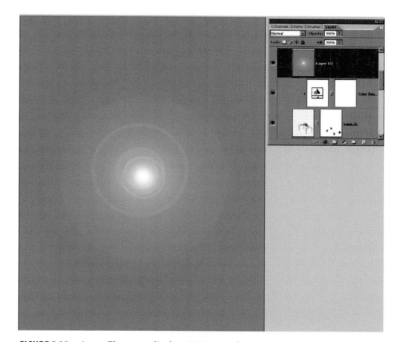

**FIGURE 5.32**  Lens Flare applied to 50% gray layer.

### Step 2

Change the 50% gray layer's blend mode to Hard Light (see Figure 5.33).

### Step 3

Resize the flare to fit the spider droid's snout, as shown in Figure 5.34.

### Step 4

Change your foreground color to yellow. Next, select the Paintbrush and change its blend mode to Dissolve (see Figure 5.35).

**FIGURE 5.33**   Change the blend mode of the lens flare layer to Hard Light.

**FIGURE 5.34**   Lens Flare resized.

## Step 5

With a soft-edge brush, paint a vertical beam starting with the snout down to the bottom of the image (see Figure 5.36).

**FIGURE 5.35**   Paint options set to Dissolve.

**FIGURE 5.36**   Particle beam applied.

## Step 6

Give the beam some Motion Blur (see Figure 5.37).

## Step 7

To add a denser core to the laser we place a rectangular selection as shown in Figure 5.38.

**FIGURE 5.37**   Motion Blur applied to particle beam.

**FIGURE 5.38**   Selection applied to particle beam.

## Step 8

Deselect the selection (Ctrl-D) and create a new layer and fill the selection with white (see Figure 5.39).

## Step 9

Apply some Gaussian Blur (Filter > Blur > Gaussian Blur), as shown in Figure 5.40.

## Step 10

Select both the layers for the laser, apply some perspective to the shape (Edit > Transform > Perspective), and rotate it approximately 45° to the left. When done, merge them (see Figures 5.41 and 5.42).

**FIGURE 5.39** Selection filled with white.

**FIGURE 5.40** Gaussian Blur applied.

**FIGURE 5.41** Perspective applied to laser.

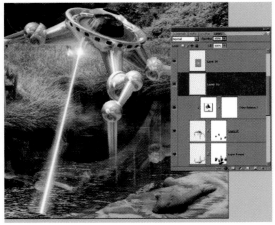

**FIGURE 5.42** Rotations applied to laser.

## Step 11

Associate a mask to the laser layer to block out the lower third of the laser. Next, duplicate the Lens Flare and place it where the laser hits the water and transform it so that it is a horizontal oval shape. Use Hue/Saturation to intensify the color (see Figure 5.43).

**FIGURE 5.43**    Further editing to the laser layer.

## Step 12

Create a new layer and paint the steam effects on it using one of the animated smoke brushes that you created in the second half of Chapter 4 (see Figure 5.44).

**FIGURE 5.44**    Apply steam.

## Step 13

Next, make the steam look as if it is rising quickly by applying a slight Motion Blur (see Figure 5.45).

**FIGURE 5.45**    Apply Motion Blur to the steam layer.

## Step 14

We will add some depth of field techniques so that the viewer's attention focuses on the spider droid. Make sure that you have selected the very top layer of the "bridge" layer set. In this case it's the adjustment layer. Simultaneously hit Ctrl-alt-shift N then hit E. This command merges all of the visible layers into a new layer above the one you had selected (see Figure 5.46).

**FIGURE 5.46**    Merge layers.

## Step 15

Next, apply Gaussian Blur to cut down on the sharpness of the image. Experiment with the settings to get what you like best (see Figure 5.47).

**FIGURE 5.47**    Apply Gaussian Blur.

## Step 16

Now we will apply the depth of field. Create a Gradient Mask to the Gaussian Blur layer where white dominates the top and graduates to black at the bottom (see Figures 5.48 and 5.49).

ON THE CD

Now you will add the finishing touches to the image. On the CD-ROM go to Tutorial/ch 5 landscape and open reflection 2.tif. You are going to add another reflection that shows the belly of the spider droid. The others worked well because they were duplicates of the original shape but they did not show the underbelly of the droid. Place it underneath the spider droid layer and add a mask. Edit the mask with your Paintbrush so that only the circular underbelly shows through. In addition, duplicate your laser layer and flip it vertically to include it as a reflection as well.

FIGURE 5.49    View of the Gradient Mask.

FIGURE 5.48    Apply a Gradient Mask to the Gaussian Blur layer.

## Step 17

Access the nik Color Efex Pro 2.0 Selective and choose Graduated Neutral Density, as shown in Figures 5.50 and 5.51.

Once the filter is applied, reduce the opacity, as shown in Figures 5.52 and 5.53.

FIGURE 5.50    nik Color Efex Pro 2.0 Selective.

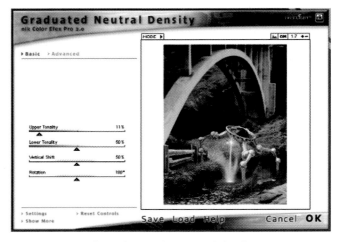

FIGURE 5.51    Graduated Neutral Density dialog box.

**FIGURE 5.52**    Graduated Neutral Density applied.

**FIGURE 5.53**    Graduated Neutral Density image reduced in opacity.

ON THE CD

Look ahead to Figure 5.62 to see the final image of our tutorial; however, another version of the bridge is included on the CD-ROM in the `Tutorials/ch 5 landscape` folder. It's called `Bridge 2.crw`. Figure 5.61 shows a version using that one. If you feel a little ambitious try this tutorial with both versions. But before we conclude it is a good idea to get some quick insight into how the reflections were applied to the 3D model.

## REFLECTIONS APPLIED IN LIGHTWAVE 8

Keep in mind that this book is not deeply involved with 3D. However, this section provides some possibilities of what can be done with LightWave to enhance your work.

The 3D environment is a challenging one. Not only do we have to be concerned with the x and y coordinates, which most of us already understand as 2D space, but also we need to be aware of the z axis that defines depth. This is the axis that throws most 2D artists off. The wonderful thing about 3D space is that we can specify textures and details anywhere on our model. The following shows how we achieved the 3D effects of the spider droid. Figure 5.54 is a view of our model in 3D space.

In LightWave there is an option to apply images as reflections to any surface of a 3D model. A jpeg image was made of the bridge landscape and imported into LightWave's compositing engine located in the Effects panel (see Figure 5.55).

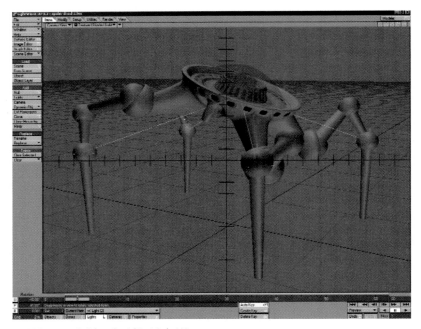

**FIGURE 5.54** Spider droid in LightWave.

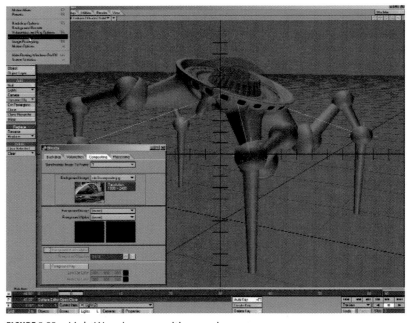

**FIGURE 5.55** LightWave's compositing engine.

Once the necessary data is loaded, the Image World command is activated. This takes the Jpeg image of the bridge scene and maps it around the 3D object to be reflected onto its surface (see Figure 5.56).

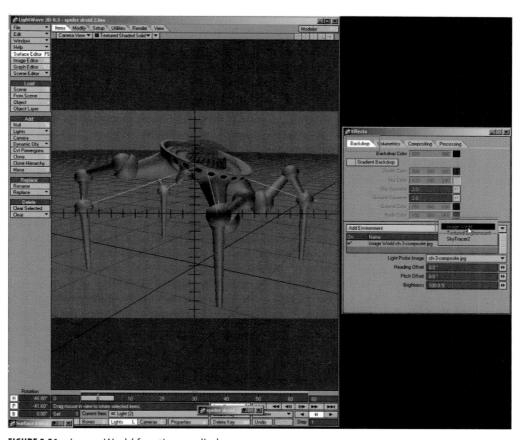

**FIGURE 5.56**    Image World function applied.

All that's left to do is to tell LightWave what surfaces we want this to reflect in. Hit F5 to activate the surface panel where you can view all of the surface attributes. The surface we are interested in is the one that will represent the silvery outer surface of the spider droid. That surface is called Base and it has a reflection property of 74%. This tells us that the base surface will reflect the background onto its surface at 74% strength (see Figure 5.57).

Hit F9 to render the image. The background image has been condensed to fit the view of the camera dimensions but that is okay because all we care about is retrieving the object with the colors of the scene reflecting into the surface (see Figure 5.58).

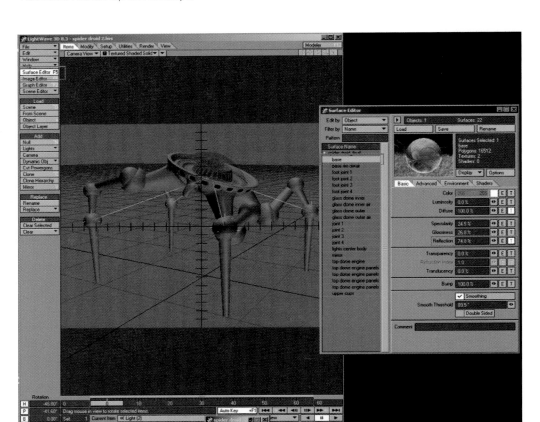

**FIGURE 5.57**  Surface properties.

**FIGURE 5.58**  Rendered image.

We can save our image in a variety of formats in the panel of the rendered image. We will choose the TGA format because it will export with its own alpha channel (see Figure 5.59). Save the image to anywhere on your hard drive (see Figure 5.60).

**FIGURE 5.59**    Rendered image is exported.

**FIGURE 5.60**    Save the image to your hard drive.

As we have done, you can import the image into Photoshop to apply other creative alternatives, like the ones we achieved in this tutorial, and as you can see in Figures 5.61 and 5.62. Take your time and have fun.

**FIGURE 5.61**    Alternative bridge view.

**FIGURE 5.62**    Final image.

## STARSHIP FLIGHT

This should be a fun exercise. We will take two 3D models created in LightWave and build a scene where they will be destroying a distant meteor. To be resourceful, we will use one of the meteors that we created in Chapter 4. As the ships fire upon it, it will break up into chunks of exploding rock.

This chapter is also an exercise in using images unpredictably because we will use images differently from how you might think they should be used. Let's blow some stuff up!

### Step 1

ON THE CD

Open `cavern.tif` from the `Tutorials/ch 5 starship flight` folder on the CD-ROM (see Figure 5.63).

### Step 2

Duplicate the layer and apply some Zoom Blur (Filter > Blur > Radial Blur), as shown in Figure 5.64.

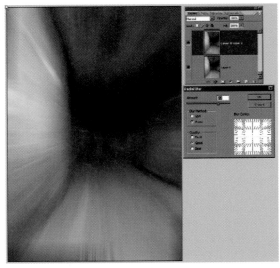

**FIGURE 5.63**   Cavern.tif opened.

**FIGURE 5.64**   Apply Zoom Blur.

## Step 3

The next step is to move the center portion of the blur effect toward the upper right corner of the composition. Use Warp (Edit > Transform > Warp) to achieve this. This allows
you to move the center by distorting the mesh so that its center shifts to the upper right,
thus maintaining the position of the frame. This mesh works like the Bezier Pen tool.
Move the points and the curve to assist you with your goal (see Figure 5.65).

**FIGURE 5.65**   Use Warp to move
the center portion of the image.

## Step 4

Give some depth to the cavern by applying a Curve adjustment layer. Edit the mask so that the darker tonality is restricted to the center section (see Figure 5.66).

## Step 5

ON THE CD

Access `star cruiser 1.tif` located in the `Tutorials/ch 5 starship flight` folder and drag the image into the file (see Figure 5.67).

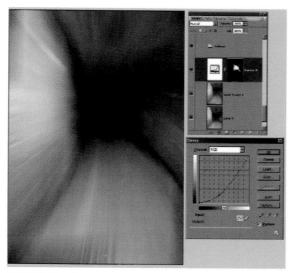

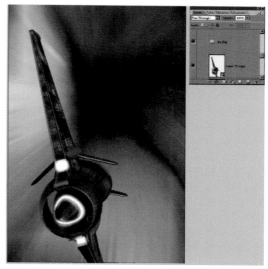

**FIGURE 5.66**    Curves adjustment layer applied.

**FIGURE 5.67**    Place Star Cruiser 1.

## Step 6

ON THE CD

Next, place and transform `star cruiser 2.tif` through `star cruiser 4.tif` files from the `Tutorial/ch 5 starship flight` folder according to Figure 5.68.

## Step 7

The ship on the far left is the farthest away, which means is should appear darker, so we will apply a Curves adjustment layer to bring down the density of the ship, as shown in Figure 5.69.

## Step 8

Apply the same Curves settings for Star Cruiser 3 (see Figure 5.70).

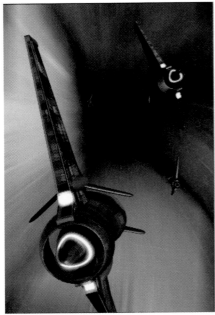

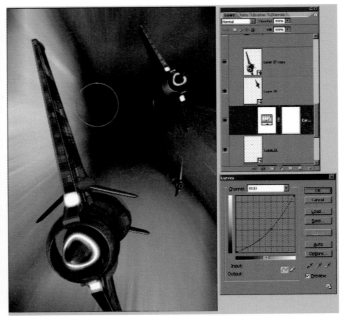

**FIGURE 5.68** Place Star Cruiser 2 through 4. **FIGURE 5.69** Curves applied to Star Cruiser 4.

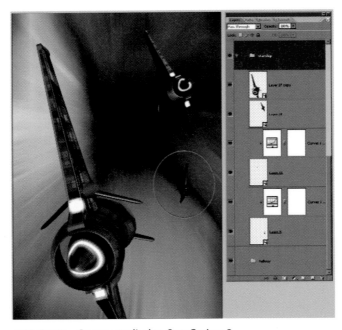

**FIGURE 5.70** Curves applied to Star Cruiser 3.

### Step 9

Duplicate the Star Cruiser 1 layer and rasterize it (see Figure 5.71).

### Step 10

Show some motion in the foreground ship. Apply Motion Blur on the duplicate layer, as shown in Figure 5.72.

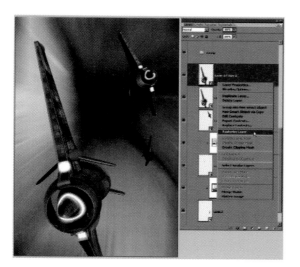

**FIGURE 5.71**    Rasterize the layer.    **FIGURE 5.72**    Apply Motion Blur.

### Step 11

Apply a mask to the Motion Blur layer to isolate it to the rear of the ship (see Figure 5.73).

### Step 12

Apply Steps 9 thru 11 for Star Cuiser 2 (see Figure 5.74).

### Step 13

Use the Lens Flare technique to apply the fiery exhaust by filling the 50% gray layer with Lens Flare (Filter > Render > Lens Flare) and changing layer blend mode to Hard Light (see Figures 5.75 and 5.76).

### Step 14

Transform the Lens Flare as shown in Figure 5.77

**FIGURE 5.73** Apply Mask to Motion Blur layer.

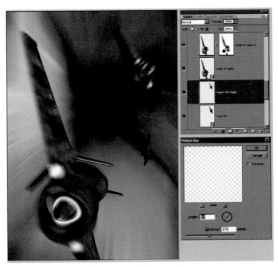

**FIGURE 5.74** Apply Motion Blur technique.

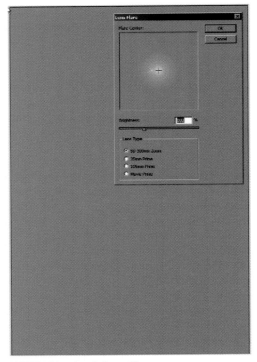

**FIGURE 5.75** Apply Lens Flare.

**FIGURE 5.76** Change layer blend mode to Hard Light.

## Step 15

Duplicate and transform the Lens Flare three times and place each one at the base of the ship's engine. Use layer masking to sculpt the exhaust to appear that it is emitting from the engine (see Figure 5.78).

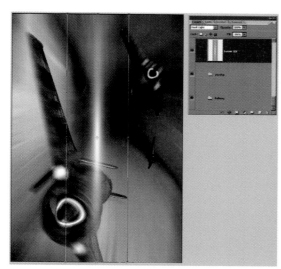

**FIGURE 5.77**    Transform Lens Flare.

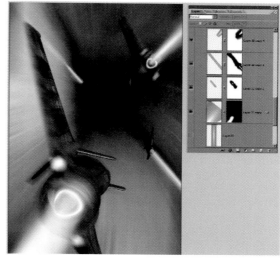

**FIGURE 5.78**    Duplicate Lens Flare.

## Step 16

Since the foreground ship is closer let's add a little more detail to the exhaust. Duplicate its Lens Flare layer and apply the Glass Filter effect. This gives us the heat wave distortion effect (see Figures 5.79 and 5.80).

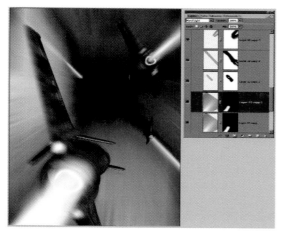

**FIGURE 5.79**    Duplicate Lens Flare.

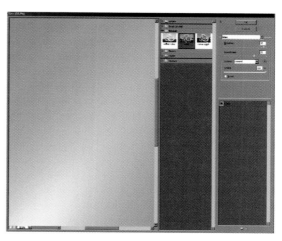

**FIGURE 5.80**    Apply Glass Filter to Lens Flare.

## Step 17

Apply levels to increase contrast and saturation. Lower its opacity and edit the mask to allow it to blend more harmoniously (see Figures 5.81 and 5.82).

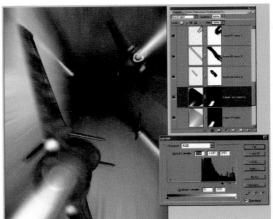

**FIGURE 5.81**   Apply levels to Lens Flare.          **FIGURE 5.82**   Layer opacity is adjusted.

## Step 18

Apply a little extra detail to the exhaust and place a green Lens Flare at the base of the ship's engine. Adjust its layer opacity to blend them (see Figure 5.83).

**FIGURE 5.83**   Apply green Lens Flare.

## APPLYING SPACE AND STAR EFFECTS

Now we will make a drastic change to the theme of the image. The concept of the ships flying through the corridor will become stars and exploding meteors.

### Step 1

Apply Infrared Thermal Color through the nik Color Efex Pro 2.0 (see Figures 5.84 through 5.86).

**FIGURE 5.84**    Apply Infrared Thermal Color.

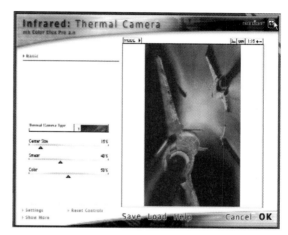

**FIGURE 5.85**    The Infrared Thermal Camera interface.

**FIGURE 5.86**    Result of applying Infrared Thermal Color in Step 1.

## Step 2

Place this below the ships in a layer set called "space," as shown in Figure 5.87.

**FIGURE 5.87** Reposition the Infrared Thermal Color layer.

## Step 3

Create a new layer and fill it with stars. There are a variety of ways to achieve this. In Chapter 4 of *Photoshop CS Trickery and FX*, there is an extensive tutorial on creating stars. So if you have the book, you can follow that one or use your own technique. In this example, white specks are on a black background. By changing the blend mode to Lighten, the dark tonalities become transparent revealing the stars (see Figure 5.88).

## Step 4

Make sure that your foreground and background colors are white and gray respectively. Fill a new layer with white and medium gray clouds (Filter > Render > Clouds). Next apply Polar Coordinates (Filter > Distort > Polar Coordinates). Check the Rectangle to Polar checkbox (see Figure 5.89).

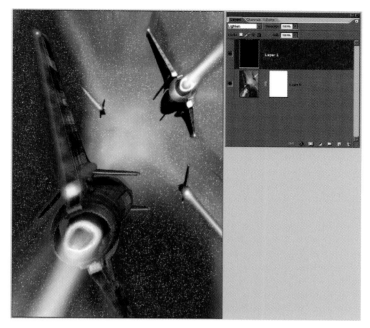

**FIGURE 5.88**    Adding stars.

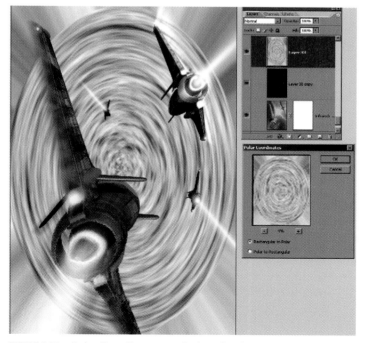

**FIGURE 5.89**    Polar Coordinates applied to clouds.

## Step 5

Change the layer's blend mode to Overlay so that only the radial-shaped values of the texture of this layer interact with the color background. This will be the start of your explosion (see Figure 5.90).

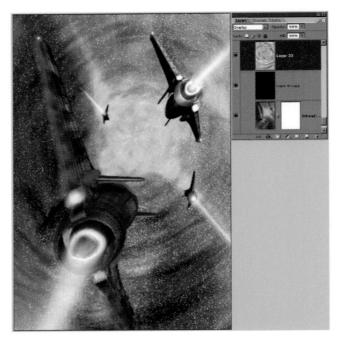

**FIGURE 5.90**     Change the blend mode of Polar Coordinates layer to Overlay.

## Step 6

Now modify the image to give the scene greater depth. Apply two adjustment layers. Apply Hue/Saturation to give it a slight desaturated effect so that the color will not drag the viewer's attention away from the ship. Apply Levels to add contrast and richness. Use the following settings as starting points only (see Figures 5.91 and 5.92).

## Step 7

At this stage feel free to add additional Lens Flares for stars or color effects painted on separate layers with blend modes applied to enhance your scene, as shown in Figure 5.93.

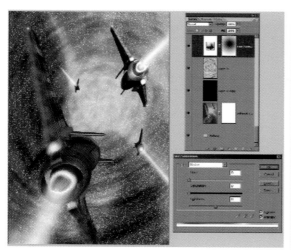

**FIGURE 5.91**    Hue/Saturation applied.

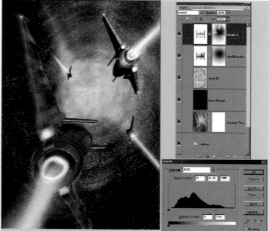

**FIGURE 5.92**    Levels applied.

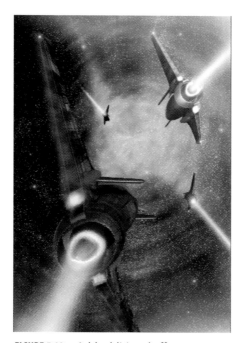

**FIGURE 5.93**    Add additional effects.

## ADDING METEORS AND EXPLOSIONS

In the final stage we will add meteors and explosions. These will be the center of interest for the background composition. The viewer's eye will catch the detailed ship in the foreground, travel to the secondary ship to the right, and its laser will guide them right to the explosion. Let's complete the tutorial.

### Step 1

ON THE CD

Place `stone-1.tif` from the `Tutorials/ch 5 starship flight` folder into a new layer below the ships and above the stars layer set (see Figure 5.94).

### Step 2

Since it will be in the background it will be much darker because it is backlit by the exploding nova, so alter its contrast using Levels directly on the layer (see Figure 5.95).

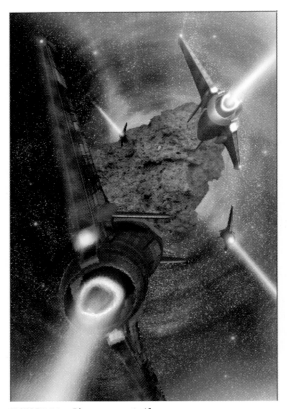

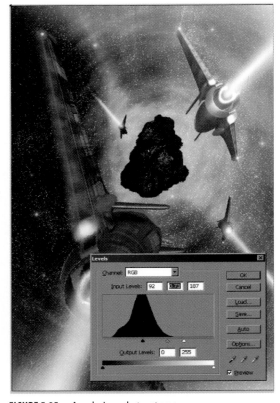

**FIGURE 5.94**    Place stone 1.tif.

**FIGURE 5.95**    Apply Levels to stone.

## Step 3

Use your Lasso tool to select and break up the meteor into pieces using cut (Ctrl-X) and paste (Ctrl-V). Additionally, duplicate some of the meteors and place them in other locations on your image. Add some Motion Blur to each to give them a sense of movement (see Figure 5.96).

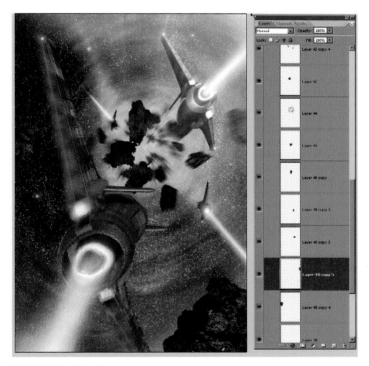

**FIGURE 5.96**    Break meteor apart.

## Step 4

Add one more layer set above all of the others and call it "explosions." Use two vibrant colors for the foreground and background colors and paint over the meteor using the smoke brushes. Continually experiment with changing the blend modes of your brush to get a variety of color interactions. When you are finished, apply some Zoom Blur (Filter > Blur > Radial Blur) to offer a sense of outward movement. Additionally, consider painting on several layers to control the result (see Figure 5.97).

Figure 5.98 shows the final result.

**FIGURE 5.97**    Create explosions.

## WHAT YOU HAVE LEARNED

- How to utilize the animated brush engine to custom create explosions
- FX tricks to create motion
- How to use Lens Flare to create exhaust
- Compositional placement of objects to guide the viewer's eye
- How to use tone to create depth

**FIGURE 5.98**    Final result.

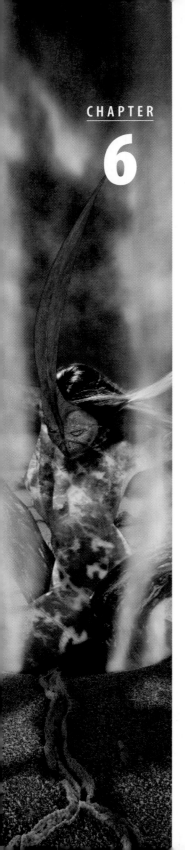

# INTEGRATING 3D OBJECTS INTO PHOTOGRAPHY

**IN THIS CHAPTER**

- Custom-creating clouds
- Creative uses for reflections
- Using filters to create depth
- Creative applications of nik Color Efex Pro 2.0

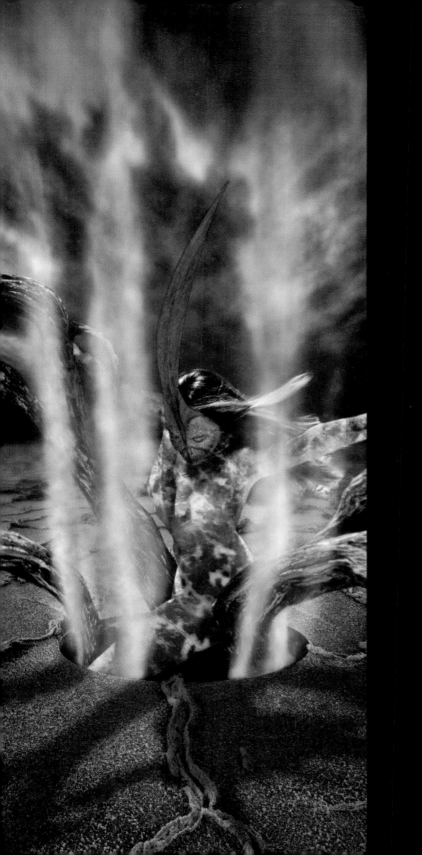

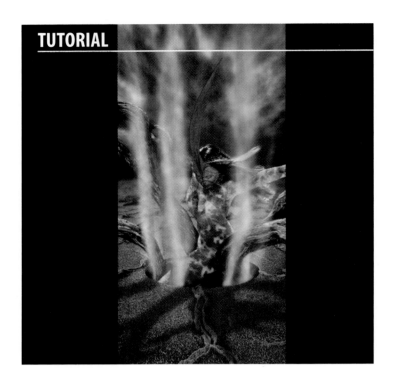

## CREATING THE INITIAL LANDSCAPE

In this exercise we will combine three different landscape-type images to serve as a backdrop for the emerging figure coming forth from beneath the depths. We will start by combining the landscape image. Then we will add custom-created clouds to enhance the scene. Next we will add the human figure, which we will later clothe in a series of textures. This will be fun, but be patient and take your time.

### Step 1

ON THE CD

Create a 2 × 5-inch file with a resolution of 300 ppi. Access the `Tutorials/ch 6 emergence` folder on the CD-ROM and open `devils-golf-course.tif`, `death-valley-race-track.tif`, and `sunset.tif`.

Since you are already familiar with layer masking, Figure 6.1 shows the completed results. However, we'll quickly review the procedure.

Blend the three images by placing devils-golf-course as the top layer, death-valley-race-track below it, and sunset on the bottom. Now use your layer masking to produce something that resembles Figure 6.1.

When it's complete, merge the layers so that you can continue to work on a single layer (see Figure 6.1).

## Step 2

Now it's time to create the opening in the ground. Associate a layer mask to the newly merged background layer. Outline a small area that is one-third of the way up from the bottom with the Elliptical Marquee tool and fill the mask with black (see Figure 6.2).

**FIGURE 6.1**  Portrait on the beach.

**FIGURE 6.2**  Hole made in the ground.

## Step 3

Add some depth to the sides of the hole. Duplicate the background layer. Select the layer below and with your Move tool activated nudge the lower layer down by hitting your down arrow key a few strokes to offset the two. Ctrl-click on the mask of the layer above to get a selection. Now hit Ctrl-shift-I to invert the selection. Hit delete on the keyboard to give this image a hole. Access your Move tool and nudge the lower layer down by 10 pixels by hitting the down arrow key on your keyboard to offset the two layers. Give this a little Motion Blur and change the contrast so that the two layers are distinctly different. This now gives the illusion that there is depth along the edge (see Figure 6.3).

## Step 4

Create a new layer below the background and fill it with black to give the hole a sense of depth. Now place some of the ground texture from the death-valley-race-track image above the black-filled layer to be seen through the hole. Reduce its opacity so that you maintain depth but that you also see a hint of texture (see Figure 6.4).

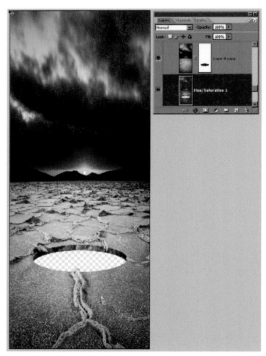

**FIGURE 6.3**    Hole edge created.

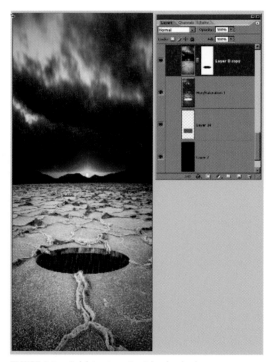

**FIGURE 6.4**    Add texture inside the hole.

## Step 5

Give the entire scene a little more richness through the use of Curves and Levels adjustment layers (see Figures 6.5 and 6.6).

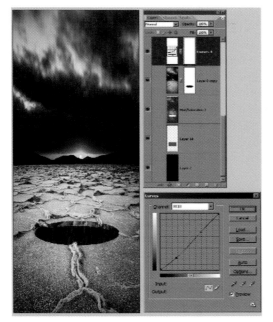

**FIGURE 6.5**    Curves adjustment layer.

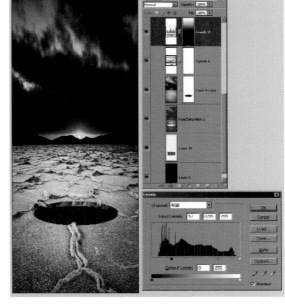

**FIGURE 6.6**    Levels adjustment layer.

### Step 6

This is a good time to place everything into a layer set. In this example it's called "landscape" (see Figure 6.7).

### Step 7

Fill a new layer with 50% gray and white clouds (Filter > Render > Clouds). Change blend mode to Overlay so that you will see only the white. Use Perspective (Edit > Transform > Perspective) to allow the clouds to appear to the viewer that the clouds are forward (see Figure 6.8).

### Step 8

Your goal is to create a sunset reflecting on the clouds. To do this you will need to add more clouds to represent the color scheme of the sunset in the background. Recreate Step 7 in four more layers, but instead of using white, use your Eyedropper tool to select a shade of red and use this color for one of the cloud layers. Red has a tendency to dominate so create a cloud layer using black to add some depth to the scene. Use the top two layers to add different variations on the clouds by using different cloud patterns using white. Their brightness will assist in creating the illusion that the clouds are coming forward. This works in tandem with the black clouds to create the depth. Transform each layer differently to achieve a more spontaneous look. Reduce

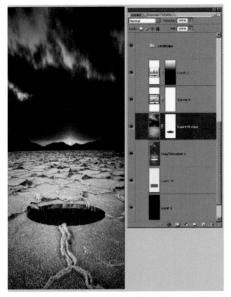

**FIGURE 6.7**    Place layers in "landscape" layer set.

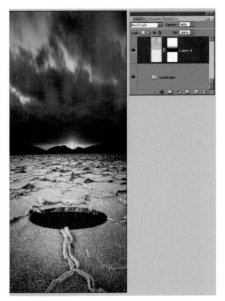

**FIGURE 6.8**    Create clouds.

the opacities of all the layers to get what you like best. Experiment! (See Figures 6.9 through 6.12.)

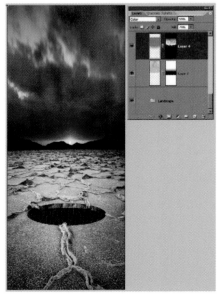

**FIGURE 6.9**    Create clouds using more colors.

**FIGURE 6.10**    Transform each color to get a natural look.

**FIGURE 6.11**   Reduce the opacities of the layers.

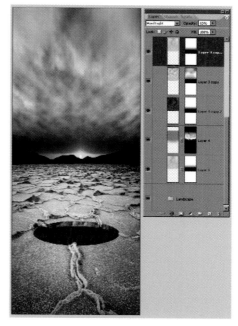

**FIGURE 6.12**   Experiment to create clouds as shown in Step 8.

## Step 9

Give the upper one-third section of the image a little more density. Use a Levels adjustment layer to achieve this. In addition, apply a Gradient Mask to isolate its effects to the top one-third of the image, as shown in Figure 6.13.

## Step 10

ON THE CD

Place the `portrait.tif` from the `Tutorial/ch 6 emergence` folder into the scene and position the figure above the opening you created (see Figure 6.14).

## Step 11

Edit the figure's layer mask to isolate the body and the main tree trunks from the background, as shown in Figure 6.15.

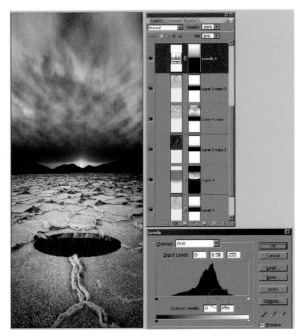

**FIGURE 6.13** Apply a Levels adjustment layer.

**FIGURE 6.14** Place portrait.

**FIGURE 6.15** Edit the mask.

## Step 12

Now you will extend the tree to the edge of the frame on the left and add an additional tree stump coming out of the hole. Start by selecting a portion of the existing limb from the lower right corner and pasting it into place as shown in Figure 6.16. Use Free Transform (Ctrl-t) and Distort (Edit > Transform > Distort) to line them up as close as you can with the initial tree branch. Use layer masking to assist you in shaping the limbs. Use your Clone tool with a soft-edge brush to cover up the edges that resulted from the cut-and-paste technique in order to integrate them as one solid piece. With your clone tool activated, Alt-click on a portion of the tree trunk and clone over the torn edges. Adjust the brush edge by use of Shift-[ for a soft-edge brush or Shift-] for a hard-edge brush.

## Step 13

ON THE CD

Access the Chapter 6 Emergence folder in the Tutorials folder of the CD-ROM and open `leaf-1.tif` and `leaf-2.tif`. Place them over the portrait layer. Change their blend mode to Hard Light and position each one over different areas of the model. Duplicate the leaf layers to give yourself greater control over placement and use Layer masks to isolate the texture to the body of the model. Use the leaf-1 with a mask to restrict its detail to the face and neck region (see Figure 6.17). Use a soft-edge Paintbrush to add the texture to the body.

**FIGURE 6.16**   Clone the tree trunk extensions.

**FIGURE 6.17**   Body detail with leaves.

*You can also use the mask you created in Step 11 to isolate the model's body by Alt-dragging the mask on top of the leaves to get things started.*

## Step 14

Merge the texture into its own layer (Ctrl-alt-shift then hit N then E). Apply a Hue/Saturation and Selective color adjustment layer. Use Figures 6.18 and 6.19 as starting examples, then experiment on your own.

**FIGURE 6.18**    Hue/Saturation adjustment layer.

## Step 15

Bring in the leaf-1.tif again and use the Warp command to transform it into the head-dress, as shown in Figure 6.20. Figure 6.21 shows the completed headdress.

   The overall image appears to be a little flat tonally so let's use Curves to increase contrast and Hue/Saturation to punch up the color a bit. In addition, add some steam coming from underneath with the use of one of the smoke brushes that you used in Chapters 3 and 4. Make sure that you add a little Motion Blur to the smoke to give it a sense of movement. See our final results in Figure 6.22.

**FIGURE 6.19**    Selective color adjustment layer.

**FIGURE 6.20**    Headdress
detail with red leaf.

**FIGURE 6.21**    Headdress
completed.

**FIGURE 6.22**    Final image.

## Creating the Reflections

We will create a surrealistic scene. Using a simple doorway image, we will replace the floor with a watery environment. Through the doorway we will place another scene of an ocean landscape. Floating over the ocean landscape will be another doorway opening up to another scene. That doorway will reflect in the water of the first entryway. Let's begin.

### Step 1

ON THE CD

Create a new file that is 10 × 12 inches with a resolution of 300 ppi (RGB). Access the ch 6 reflections folder in the Tutorials folder of the CD-ROM and open entry way.tif. Drag this image into the new file and resize it (see Figure 6.23).

### Step 2

You will not need the doorway area so use the rectangular Marquee tool to cut out the doorway. Duplicate this layer (Ctrl-J) and invert it vertically (Edit > Transform > Flip Vertically). Next, apply the glass filter (Filter > Distort > Glass), as shown in Figure 6.24.

**FIGURE 6.23**   Create a new file.

### Step 3

Change the opacity to 32% and position it so that the base of the wall lines up, as shown in Figure 6.25.

### Step 4

Now we will change the nature of the door by adding some texture to it. We will also add its reflection.

ON THE CD

Access the ch 6 reflections folder in the Tutorials folder of the CD-ROM and open door texture.tif. Use Free Transform (Ctrl-T) to line it up over the door. Reduce its opacity to around 41% to blend with the door. Next, duplicate this texture, inverse it vertically, and place it below the base of the door to create the reflection of the texture (see Figure 6.26).

### Step 5

Now let's add the outside world behind the doorway.

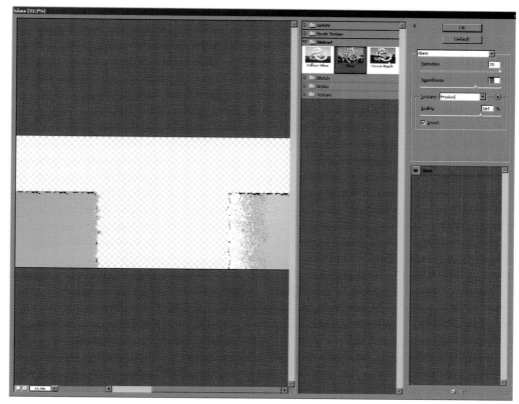

**FIGURE 6.24**    Duplicate the doorway and apply the glass filter.

**FIGURE 6.25**    Reduce the opacity.

**FIGURE 6.26**    Create the reflection of the texture.

Access the ch 6 reflections folder in the Tutorials folder of the CD-ROM and open seascape.tif. Place it so that the water fills the room and the horizon line sets one-third of the way up from the base of the door. Use Free Transform (Ctrl-T) to accomplish this. Reduce its opacity to around 41% to blend with the door. Next, apply a mask to isolate the water to the doorway (see Figure 6.27).

**FIGURE 6.27**    Apply seascape.

## Step 6

Add a Curves adjustment layer to reduce the tones to a brighter gray. This will serve as a great backdrop for the next step (see Figure 6.28).

**FIGURE 6.28**    Apply Curves.

## Step 7

Use your selection tools to cut and paste the door frame into a separate layer. Use the original doorway layer to copy from (see Figure 6.29).

Double click on the blank portion on the right side of the door frame to access the Layer Effects panel. Apply Bevel and Emboss to give the edges some depth (see Figure 6.30).

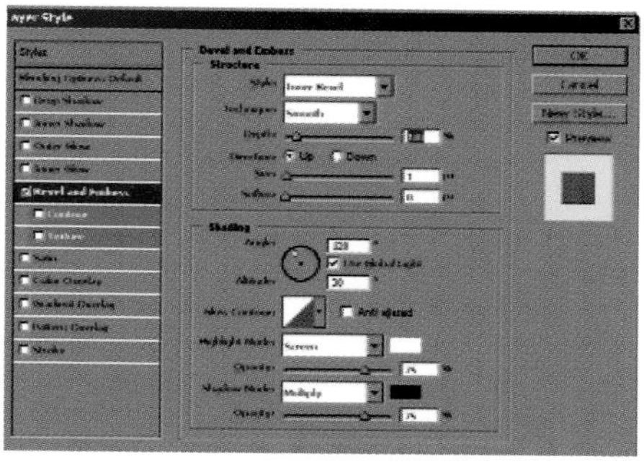

**FIGURE 6.30**    Apply Bevel and Emboss.

**FIGURE 6.29**    Create doorway edge.

Now we will add a slight glow to help the doorway stand out more effectively. Create a new layer above the door frame and make a rectangular selection around it. Stroke it with white (Edit > Stroke > Stroke with white) on the inside of the selection and give it a slight Gaussian Blur (Filter > Blur > Gaussian Blur), as shown in Figure 6.31.

## Step 8

Now duplicate the doorway layer again and resize it (Ctrl-T) to fit inside of the door frame. This is now a floating doorway. Merge the doorway and the door frame (see Figure 6.32).

## Step 9

Give the floating doorway some increased contrast to achieve greater depth. Apply a Curves adjustment layer and lock it to the floating doorway (see Figure 6.33).

**FIGURE 6.31**   Add glow.

**FIGURE 6.32**   Resize the doorway to fit into the frame.

**FIGURE 6.33**   Apply contrast with Curves.

## Step 10

Let's create the reflection for the floating doorway. Duplicate the doorway and invert it vertically (Edit > Transform > Inverse Vertically). Reduce its shape and place it over the watery interior beneath the doorway. Next, reduce its opacity to around 42%. Since reflections are denser in tonality than their real counterparts, reduce the brightness by applying a Curves adjustment layer (see Figure 6.34).

## Step 11

The center of focus is really the floating door, so richen the tonality with the use of a Curves adjustment layer. Edit the mask so that the effect will not touch the sky portions of the doorway, as shown in Figure 6.35.

**FIGURE 6.34**    Apply contrast with Curves.

**FIGURE 6.35**    Apply density with Curves.

When complete, use the Hue/Saturation adjustment layer and reduce the saturation to more of a black-and-white look. Figure 6.36 shows that the floating doorway stands out well.

**FIGURE 6.36**    Apply Hue/Saturation.

## Step 12

The doorway looks great, but let's see if we can enhance it further. Access the Pro Contrast in nik Color Efex Pro 2.0 (see Figure 6.37).

Play with the Pro Contrast settings but use Figure 6.38 as a reference.

**FIGURE 6.37**    Access Pro Contrast.

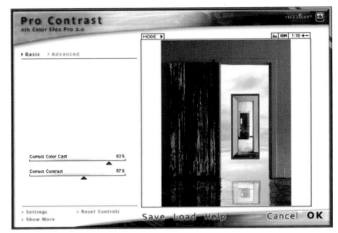

**FIGURE 6.38**    Pro Contrast dialog box.

## Step 13

Finally, mask out the effects of the Pro Contrast filter from the doorway. This allows the warmth of the floating doorway to become more prominent (see Figure 6.39). Figure 6.40 shows the finished piece.

**FIGURE 6.39**    Mask out the door.

**FIGURE 6.40**    Finished result of Step 13.

## WHAT YOU HAVE LEARNED

- How to create depth by altering Color and Saturation
- How to use creative applications of nik Color Efex Pro 2.0
- How to use creative approaches for reflections
- How to use simplicity to create compelling imagery

# WORKING WITH PEOPLE AND BACKGROUNDS

**IN THIS CHAPTER**

- Turning portraits into ceramic objects
- Custom-creating clouds
- Using textures to blend with human skin
- Using masks to isolate a person
- Adding animal attributes to a human

## CREATING THE BACKGROUND AND MASK

In this exercise we will transform a simple head shot into a ceramic mask floating over a watery landscape. We will start by creating the background, and then we will edit the head shot.

### Step 1

ON THE CD

Create a file that is 10 × 12 inches with a resolution of 300 ppi. Access the `Tutorial/ch 7 cracked head` folder on the CD-ROM, drag in `cloud.tif`, and place it in the upper half of the composition, as shown in Figure 7.1. Use Free Transform if you need to. Underneath this layer create a new layer and fill it with black. Next, apply a little contrast to the mountain range by applying a Curves adjustment layer and edit out the background by filling the mask with black and painting the mountain area with white to restrict the effect of the Curves adjustment to the mountain range.

Place these layers into a layer set titled "background." Turn off the clouds for now, but allow the black background to stay visible.

**FIGURE 7.1**    Place cloudscape.

### Step 2

ON THE CD

Access the Tutorial/ch 7 cracked head folder and drag in portrait.tif. Place it in a layer set above the background titled "portrait" (see Figure 7.2).

### Step 3

Remove the hair by using the Clone Stamp tool. Use the skin as the source and slowly shape the head. Make sure that you use a soft-edge brush. In addition, you are going to cut out and re-texture most of the head so do not spend a lot of time trying to get it perfect. Alt-click on the skin portions of the portrait and clone it over the hair. The goal is to get a fleshy overlay for most of the head. This is the beginning of the mask (see Figure 7.3).

*You could do this by painting with the color of the skin tone, however you may lose the original texture that was captured by the camera.*

**FIGURE 7.2** Portrait.

**FIGURE 7.3** Remove hair.

## Step 4

Use the Pencil tool to plan out how the face will be cracked. Draw on a separate layer above your head. This approach allows you to outline more freely. Use Figure 7.4 as a guide, however feel free to make your own designs.

 *You may end up creating several versions, but be patient. Also, consider using broken glass or egg shells for inspiration.*

## Step 5

Use your Pen tool to follow the outlines that you drew (see Figure 7.5). This will give you more control of the outlines in the end.

## Step 6

First, apply a Layer mask to the portrait. Next, in your Path Palette (Windows > Path) find a thumbnail of the outline that you just created. Ctrl-click on the thumbnail to create a selection. Edit the mask so that the left side of the face disappears. Edit the mask to remove the socket (see Figure 7.6).

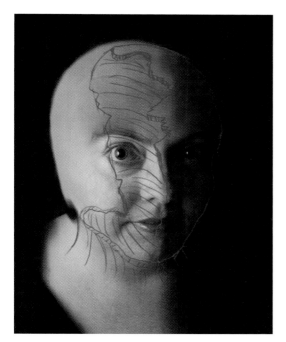

**FIGURE 7.4**    Draw outlines.

**FIGURE 7.5**    Apply the Pen tool to outlines.

**FIGURE 7.6**    Apply a Layer mask.

### Step 7

Access the `Tutorial/ch 7 cracked head` folder and drag in `texture 1.tif` underneath the portrait. Use the Layer effect to create a Gradient Overlay. Follow the parameters in Figure 7.7. Give the texture a Layer mask to isolate it to the left side of the face.

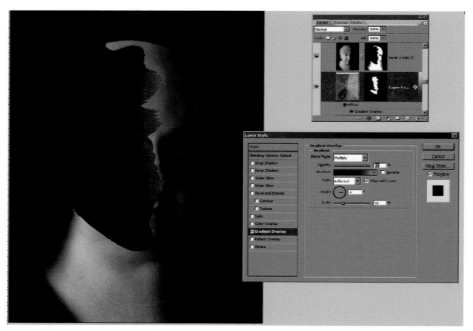

**FIGURE 7.7** Apply a Layer mask.

### Step 8

Duplicate the portrait layer and place it underneath the texture. Add noise (Filter > Noise > Add Noise) and give it some Motion Blur (Filter > Blur > Motion Blur), as shown in Figure 7.8.

Apply a mask and fill it with black to block out the image. Edit the mask with white paint in the eye socket to simulate thickness for the walls of the mask (see Figure 7.9).

Duplicate this layer again but this time add the rear frame to the mask, as shown in Figure 7.10.

Duplicate this layer one last time and add the thickness to the side of the face, as shown in Figure 7.11.

**FIGURE 7.8**    Noise and Motion Blur.

**FIGURE 7.9**    Creating the eye socket.

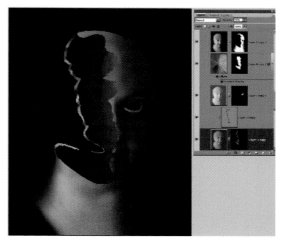

**FIGURE 7.10**    Add the rear frame.

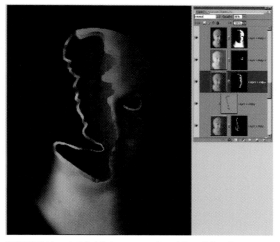

**FIGURE 7.11**    Add thickness to the side of the face.

## Step 9

ON THE CD

Access the `Tutorial/ch 7 cracked head` folder and drag in `texture 2.tif`. Add the crackling paint texture to the edge borders. Use layer masking as you did in Step 7 to achieve this (see Figure 7.12).

### Step 10

Duplicate the head shot layer and edit the mask so that the eye is visible. Hold the Alt key and select Merge Visible in the layers submenu. Now this image is in one layer. Turn off the visible properties for now; we will use this for the reflection later (see Figure 7.13).

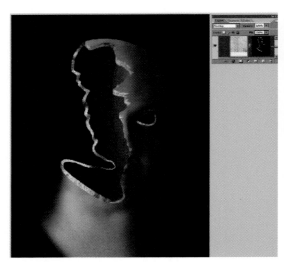

**FIGURE 7.12**    Add texture to the edges.

**FIGURE 7.13**    Make the eye visible.

### Step 11

Now duplicate the texture layer you used in Step 8 and edit the mask to overlay it over the entire head (see Figure 7.14).

### Step 12

We will make the edges more distinct by giving them a less saturated look, so apply a Hue/Saturation adjustment layer. Reduce the saturation as shown in Figure 7.15 and edit the mask to restrict the effect to the cracked edges.

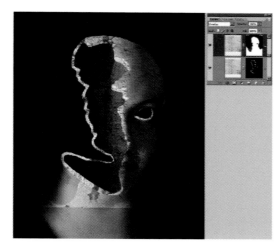

**FIGURE 7.14**    Add texture to the mask.

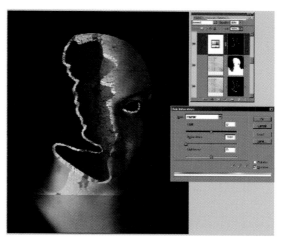

**FIGURE 7.15**    Reduce the saturation.

### Step 13

Now we will make the water that the mask will sit in. Make sure that your foreground and background colors consist of a light blue and a dark blue hue. Create a new layer and fill it with the light and dark blue clouds (Filter > Render > Clouds). Next use Free Transform (Ctrl-T) to restrict it to the lower half of the layers. Use a layer mask to soften the rear edge of the water. Also use Perspective (Edit > Transform > Perspective) to make the foreground look as if it's closer. When you are finished, access the layer effects and add a Gradient Overlay to allow the rear portion to become more luminous than the foreground (see Figure 7.16).

### Step 14

Next, turn on the background clouds that you turned off in Step 1 (see Figure 7.17).

### Step 15

Duplicate the cloud layer and place it in a layer set titled "levitating clouds." Edit the mask to allow the clouds to appear as if they are extending from the inside of the mask. Use several duplicates if you like for more expressive clouds and just edit their masks to integrate them (see Figure 7.18).

### Step 16

It's time to turn on the reflection that was created in Step 10. Inverse it vertically (Edit > Transform > Inverse Flip) and place its base at the base of the mask, as shown in Figure 7.19.

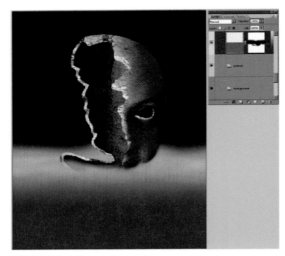

**FIGURE 7.16**    Create the water.

**FIGURE 7.17**    Turn on the background.

**FIGURE 7.18**    Create levitating clouds.

**FIGURE 7.19**    Create reflections for the mask.

## Step 17

Since the mask has a reflection, so should the clouds. Duplicate the clouds and in-verse them vertically (Edit > Transform > Flip Vertical) to create their reflections. Change their opacity to around 46% (see Figure 7.20).

## Step 18

Duplicate the clouds again to add the reflection for the entire sky. This will add a more saturated blue to the water (see Figure 7.21).

FIGURE 7.20    Create reflections for the clouds.

FIGURE 7.21    Create reflections for the sky.

## Step 19

Next, add two nik Color Efex Pro 2.0 filters. Start with the Sunshine filter and follow the settings in Figure 7.22. The result is shown in Figure 7.23. Next, apply the Bicolor Cool/Warm filter and edit its mask so that the results of the sunshine filter remain on the face (see Figures 7.24 and 7.25).

FIGURE 7.22    Add the Sunshine filter.

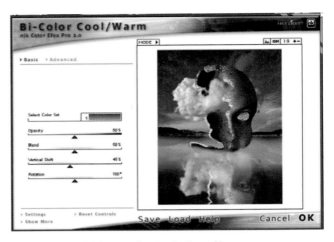

**FIGURE 7.24**    Add the Bicolor Cool/Warm filter.

**FIGURE 7.23**    Results of the Sunshine filter.

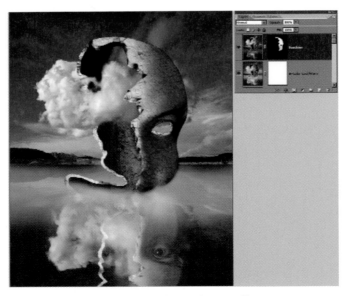

**FIGURE 7.25**    Results of the Bicolor Cool/Warm filter.

The final results, as shown in Figure 7.26, are very interesting.

**FIGURE 7.26**    Final results.

## CREATING THE WINGED WOMAN

We will transform a woman into a human/hawk hybrid. She will be poised in front of a waterfall cavern that we will create by using two different photographs. This tutorial uses Free Transform, Warp, and masking. Let's begin.

### Step 1

ON THE CD

Create a new file that is 10 × 12 inches with a resolution of 300 ppi. Access `Tutorial/ ch 7 morph` and open `sand` and `boulder.tif`. Drag this image into the new file and resize it to fit the frame (see Figure 7.27).

### Step 2

Giving an image depth from the beginning is always a helpful strategy. So we will give the foreground boulder and the one to the left more contrast and saturation. We do this by duplicating the original layer and changing the blend mode to Hard Light. This will increase the contrast and saturation of the image. Apply a black mask to this layer and apply the effect to the two stones by painting. Experiment with duplicating the layer again to apply a different blend mode to make the background even more dynamic (see Figure 7.28).

**FIGURE 7.27**    Sand and boulders.

**FIGURE 7.28**    Sand and boulders composite.

### Step 3

*ON THE CD*

Access the Tutorials/ch 7 morph folder on the CD-ROM and drag in the water fall. tif and the water fall 2.tif files. Drag in both images with water fall 2 on top. Give both layers a mask to isolate the water behind the three foreground boulders. Use water fall to fill the ground (see Figure 7.29).

### Step 4

Next, apply a little contrast change with a Curves adjustment layer to increase the overall contrast. This gives some detail to the textures. Lock the adjustment to the image by holding the Alt key while placing your mouse in between the two layers and clicking. Now the adjustment effects are isolated to the layer below it (see Figure 7.30).

### Step 5

Give a little more interest to the foreground by duplicating one of the waterfalls and transforming (Ctrl-T) to give a slightly different shape (see Figure 7.31).

### Step 6

Give this new waterfall a little more brightness by applying a Curves adjustment layer. Apply the settings as shown in Figure 7.32. Fill the mask with black and paint with white in the waterfall location (see Figure 7.32).

**FIGURE 7.29** Composite water into the background.

**FIGURE 7.30** Add a Curves adjustment layer.

**FIGURE 7.31** Add another waterfall.

**FIGURE 7.32** Add Curves to the waterfall.

## Step 7

Let's create some shallow depth of field. We will start by merging all visible layers into one independent layer (Ctrl-alt-shift-N-E). When you are done, give this layer a Gaussian Blur (Filter > Blur > Gaussian Blur). Then apply a mask to the blurred layer and give it a gradient of white at the top and black at the bottom so that the effect is less prominent in the foreground. Use Figure 7.33 as a guide.

### Step 8

Access the Tutorials/ch 7 morph folder on the CD-ROM and drag in the crouch pose.tif. Use layer masking to isolate the model. Place the woman image in a layer set titled "winged woman" (see Figure 7.34).

**FIGURE 7.33**    Apply a depth of field.

**FIGURE 7.34**    Apply the model.

To assist your masking efforts, hit the \ key when the mask is selected and see the black portions of the mask in red. This gives you the advantage of seeing the mask and the image simultaneously as you edit with the Brush tool (see Figure 7.35).

### Step 9

Access the Tutorials/ch 7 morph folder on the CD-ROM and drag in the feather detail. tif. Change its blend mode to Hard Light, apply a black mask, and edit the mask to reveal the feather detail on the model's skin. You will need to duplicate these layers several times to achieve this over the entire body (see Figure 7.36).

### Step 10

Now it's time to add the wings. Bring in the wing.tif from the Tutorial/ch 7 morph folder and position and transform it so that it extends past the model's head toward the upper-right corner (see Figure 7.37).

**FIGURE 7.35** Apply the mask.

**FIGURE 7.36** Add the feather detail.

**FIGURE 7.37** Add the wing detail.

## Step 11

Apply a mask to isolate it from its background. Use a soft-edge brush and zoom in to obtain the best results. You will create more wing details, so make a layer set for them and call it "right wing" (see Figure 7.38).

**FIGURE 7.38**    Add a mask to the wing.

## Step 12

Duplicate the wing and apply the Free Transform (Ctrl-T) and the Warp command (Edit > Transform > Warp) to curve and twist the wing toward the foreground (see Figure 7.39).

**FIGURE 7.39**    Apply Warp.

## Step 13

Duplicate the wing and apply the Hard Light blend mode. Add contrast and richness to varying areas to enhance its texture. Next, we will add shading underneath the wing, as shown in Figure 7.40.

## Step 14

Create a new layer below the series of duplicated wings that make up the one curving to the front. Fill the layer with black and give it a black-filled mask. Edit the mask with white to create the illusion of curvature to the underside of the wing. Use Figure 7.41 as a guide.

**FIGURE 7.40**    Add shading underneath the wing.

**FIGURE 7.41**    Create the illusion of curvature to the underside of the wing.

## Step 15

Now create a wing for the left side of the model using the same procedures from Steps 10 through 14. Note that you do not want the same shape of the other wing, so when you apply Warp to shape it, give the shape some variance. Place them into a layer set titled "left wing" (see Figure 7.42).

*You could just merge your original wings into a new layer and apply the Warp tool but this may not give it the spontaneity that you need. Going through each of the steps but giving them variances is a good way to protect against redundant forms.*

**Step 16**

Let's create the shadow for the figure. Merge the wings and the model into a layer and fill the pixels with black (Edit > Fill > Fill with Black). Make sure that the Preserve Transparency box is checked so that the entire layer isn't filled with black (see Figure 7.43).

**FIGURE 7.42**    Add left wing.

**FIGURE 7.43**    Create the shadow.

**Step 17**

Place the shadow layer beneath the "winged woman." The sunlight is coming from the left so use Free Transform to position the shadow on the ground to the right-hand side. Next, let's allow the shadow to flow with the contour of the stone. Use Liquefy (Filter > Liquefy) and hit W for the Forward Warp tool and push the edges of the shadow to conform to the contour of the rock. When done, click OK.

Next, apply the Warp command (Edit > Transform > Warp) to apply some global adjustments to fine-tune the flow of the shadow (see Figure 7.44).

**FIGURE 7.44** Apply Liquefy and Warp commands to mold the shadow to the contour of the rock.

## Step 18

We will use the beak from the hawk and apply it as claws for the bird woman. Select it and place it on its own layer (see Figure 7.45).

**FIGURE 7.45** Place the beak on its own layer.

## Step 19

Duplicate the beak and use Free Transform to alter the size. Additionally, use the Warp tool to alter the shape of each claw. Use layer masking to blend each claw with its designated finger. Remember to zoom in and fill the screen with the subject so that editing the mask is not a chore. Place the claws in a layer set called "claws right hand" (see Figure 7.46).

Do the same for the other hand, as shown in Figure 7.47. Place the claws in a layer set titled "claws left hand."

**FIGURE 7.47**    Create a claw for each finger of the left hand.

**FIGURE 7.46**    Create a claw for each finger of the right hand.

## Step 20

To give the woman a bird-like face, we will bring in the hawk image, as shown in Figure 7.48.

## Step 21

Apply a mask and edit to shape it. Duplicate the layer and change the blend modes as a means to alter the contrast, and saturation of the overall look and feel (see Figure 7.49).

## Step 22

To allow the winged woman to stand out in the foreground, apply a Curves adjustment layer and edit the hawk woman mask so that its effects are isolated to the winged woman (see Figure 7.50).

FIGURE 7.49    Edit the face mask.

**FIGURE 7.48**    Place the hawk image.

**FIGURE 7.50**    Apply a Curves adjustment layer.

## Step 23

The woman's red dress is visually distracting and draws too much attention, so use the settings shown in Figures 7.51 through 7.53 to make color and tonal changes to the dress. Edit one mask and then hold the Alt key and drag the mask to the other adjustment layers.

**FIGURE 7.51**    Apply the Hue/Saturation adjustment layer.

**FIGURE 7.52**    Apply the Color Balance adjustment layer.

**FIGURE 7.53**    Apply the Curves adjustment layer.

## Step 24

To complete the piece, add two nik Color Efex Pro 2.0 Filters: Sunshine and Classic Soft Focus (see Figures 7.54 and 7.55).

Let's view the final piece, as shown in Figure 7.56.

**FIGURE 7.54** Apply the Sunshine filter.

**FIGURE 7.55** Apply the Classic Soft Focus filter.

## WHAT YOU HAVE LEARNED

- How to create depth by altering Color and Saturation
- How to use creative applications of nik Color Efex Pro 2.0
- How to use creative approaches for reflections
- How to use simplicity to create compelling imagery
- How to use masking for human subjects
- How to turn portraits into ceramic objects
- How to use textures to blend with human skin
- How to use masks to isolate a person
- How to add animal attributes to a human

**FIGURE 7.56**   The final piece.

# FINE ART APPROACHES

**IN THIS CHAPTER**

- How to create a custom interior from simple textures
- How to open a door in Photoshop
- How to recreate cloud formation from photographic images
- Creative use of Liquefy
- FX tricks to create motion
- How to custom create light rays
- Using masks to isolate your subject
- Transforming layer sets

## SIPAPU

There is a new movement in art called *digital* that has allowed artists, and the public in general, to have the ability to create a unique vision in any art form via a computer. This freedom is unique to the digital medium. Today's interest in digital is breeding a new interest and vision in art, and as the computer becomes more sophisticated artists are given the tools to become more prolific and daring in what they create. A combination of photography, 3D sculpturing, painting, and scanning of 3D objects can be used in ways not seen before.

ON THE CD

In Tutorials/ch 8 sipapu you will find the source photographs of the model and the tree bark, captured with a Canon D60 digital camera, which produced a 6.1 mega pixel image. All of the leaves were scanned at a resolution of 1200 ppi with an HP Scanjet 6300 C, which produced file sizes of 30 megabytes and up. The smoke streams are 3D-rendered HyperVoxel objects created in LightWave 8.

The objects were chosen primarily for their textures; each one is unique, therefore it is challenging to decide how to utilize them to complete the final result. Let's walk through the process of creating Sipapu.

## Step 1

Let's continue the spirit of keeping everything organized in layer groups. Each one will be introduced along the way but we'll begin by creating several layer groups and title them: "light streak," "steam," "girl 1," "steam 2," and "background" (see Figure 8.1).

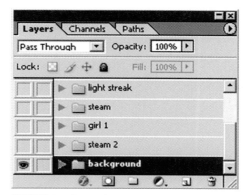

**FIGURE 8.1**    Create layer sets.

## Step 2

ON THE CD

From the CD-ROM open `tree bark.tif` in the `Tutorial/ch 8 sipapu` folder. The tree bark has an interesting biomorphic feel and it is ideal to serve as a background for the human model. After duplicating the layer (Ctrl-J) and inverting it horizontally (Edit > Transform > Flip Horizontal) use a mask to hide the seams where the two images come together. Use your Paintbrush and paint with black on the mask to make the bark go away (see Figure 8.2).

## Step 3

Create a sense of depth by allowing the viewer to focus more on the foreground areas. We will use two techniques to achieve this. First, merge everything into a new layer (Alt-ctrl-shift-N-E). All layers are merged into the new one without merging the original ones. Next, apply Gaussian Blur to the new layer because this will serve to provide the shallow depth of field (see Figure 8.3).

Associate a mask and edit it so that the blur effect is restricted mostly to the center portion of the background, as shown in Figure 8.4.

## Step 4

The background has a reddish color cast, so using a Hue/Saturation adjustment layer, pull the Saturation slider all the way to the left leaving the image black and white. Because we do not want the color to be completely taken away, edit the mask to isolate the reddish hue to the foreground areas (see Figure 8.5).

**FIGURE 8.2** Background created.

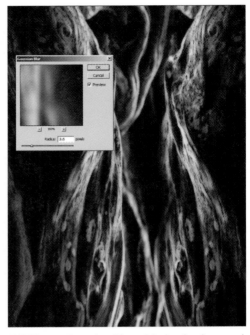

**FIGURE 8.3** Gaussian Blur added to background.

**FIGURE 8.4** Mask added to the background.

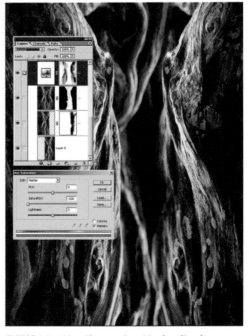

**FIGURE 8.5** Hue/Saturation Mask edited.

## Step 5

The background still has quite of bit of tonal information that could compete with the main subject matter, so we will apply a Curves adjustment layer to restrict the tonal range to deeper shades of gray. Drag the white points on the curve down to lower the highlights to a richer tone, as shown in Figure 8.6. Edit the mask to apply its effect in the center region of the background.

## Step 6

Duplicate the Curves layer to ensure that the tones are very rich and once again edit the mask to restrict the tones to the center of the image (see Figure 8.7).

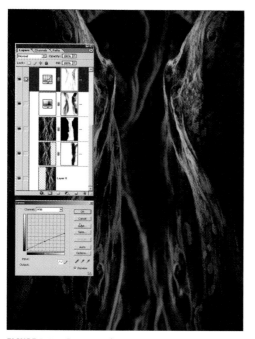

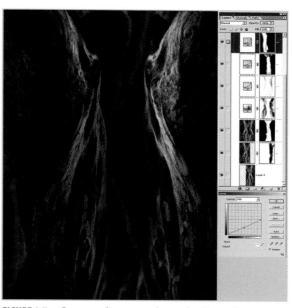

FIGURE 8.7    Curves adjustment layer duplicated.

FIGURE 8.6    Curves adjustment layer applied.

## Step 7

ON THE CD

Now we are ready to bring the model in. Access Tutorial/ch 8 sipapu and open figure.01.tif. Place her into the girl 1 layer set organized on top of the background and apply the Distort tool (Edit > Transform > Distort) to stretch her body up toward the upper right (see Figure 8.8).

**FIGURE 8.8**    Model placed in girl 1 layer set.

### Step 8

Open the figure.03.tif file in the Tutorial/ch 8 sipapu folder. Change the lower part of her body into a leaf-like figure using the Shear tool. (Filters > Distort > Shear) is used on the red leaf. Use Figure 8.9 as a guide.

### Step 9

Position the leaf to resemble a tail and add a mask. Edit the mask to mold the leaf to the model's lower body. Duplicate the leaf layer as many times as you see fit and use each one to assist you in sculpting the tail to your liking. There are no right or wrong ways to do this. Try to get as close as possible to what is shown in Figure 8.10.

### Step 10

Open the figure.02.tif and figure.04.tif files in the Tutorial/ch 8 sipapu folder. Next, apply these leaves to the body. Figure 8.11 shows how the green and yellow leaf's blend mode is set to Linear Light blend mode in one layer example. The green leaf's blend mode is set to Hue in the lower layer example. Both examples blend well with the skin and maintain the model's contour. In the next step we will discover some details about how this is initially applied.

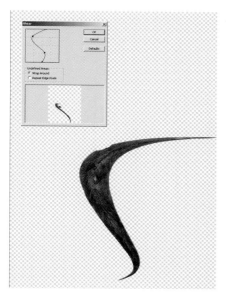

**FIGURE 8.9**    Shear applied to red leaf.

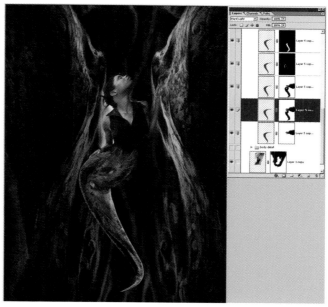

**FIGURE 8.10**    Sculpted red leaf.

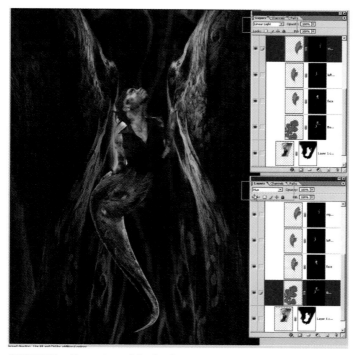

**FIGURE 8.11**    Texturing of the body.

## Step 11

Figure 8.12 shows the leaf before a mask is applied in the lower window as well as the results after the mask is edited in the main image. Use the WACOM tablet for editing the mask.

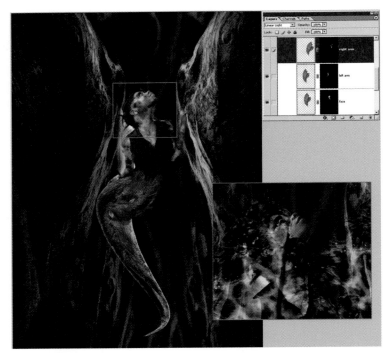

**FIGURE 8.12**    Texturing detail of the green and yellow leaf.

## Step 12

Here are the results of the green leaf when applied. Notice how the mask is edited to allow the green hue to dominate only in selected regions. Try to do the same and be patient. Start with lower opacity settings when you start editing the mask and build the effect slowly (see Figure 8.13).

## Step 13

In the same way that you created the tail in Step 8, add the red leaf to the head of the model to represent her hair. Place these layers into the Head Set folder (see Figure 8.14).

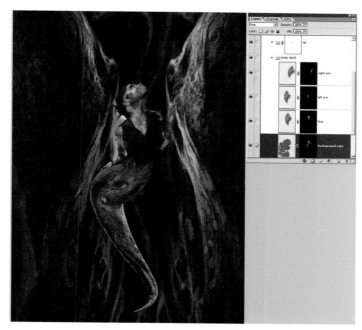

**FIGURE 8.13**    Texturing detail of the green leaf.

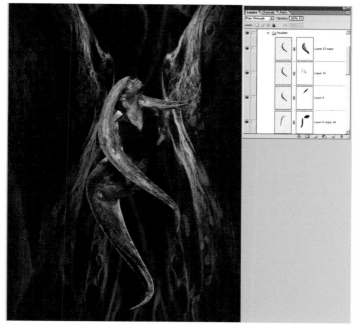

**FIGURE 8.14**    Head detail with the red leaf.

### Step 14

ON THE CD

Access the Tutorials/ch 8 sipapu folder on the CD-ROM and place brown leaf.tif into the file. Restrict its textures to the model's upper body to form a type of clothing unique from the original. Finally, use the kelp to form the collar (see Figure 8.15).

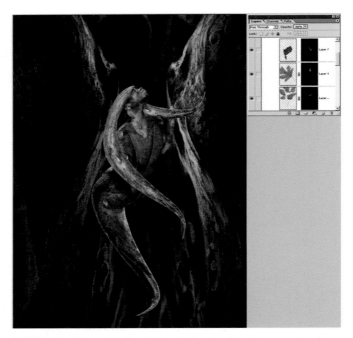

**FIGURE 8.15** Brown leaf and dried kelp detail in the upper body.

### Step 15

The brown leaf was successful for the upper body, so we will use it as an additional composite for her face and neck region, but this time we will change the blend mode to Overlay. Figure 8.16 is an example without the mask applied.

Figure 8.17 is an example of the brown leaf with the mask edited to restrict its detail to the face and neck region.

### Step 16

ON THE CD

From the CD-ROM, open smoke 6.tif and smoke 7.tif in the Tutorials/ch 8 sipapu folder. Now it's time to bring in the smoke streams that we rendered in LightWave 8. The two images were rendered and saved as Tiffs so that the smoke would be rendered onto a transparent background. Once the layer is placed, resize and duplicate it to compose the steamy smoke streams around the model. Place these images into the

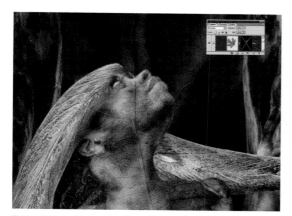

**FIGURE 8.16**    Brown leaf applied to face and neck.

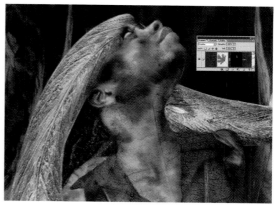

**FIGURE 8.17**    Brown leaf applied to face and neck with the mask applied.

steam 2 layer set that is positioned just above the background layer set but below the girl 1 folder. Later you will see the details for creating the smoke streams with Hyper-voxels in LightWave 8 (see Figure 8.18).

**FIGURE 8.18**    Smoke streams with the mask applied.

## Step 17

Add more of the smoke streams but this time place them into the steam layer set, which is positioned above the girl 1 folder. Change the blend mode to Screen to enhance the whites. Now the effect is more steam than smoke (see Figure 8.19).

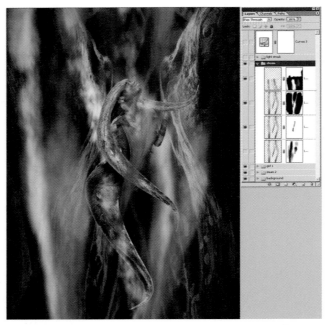

**FIGURE 8.19**   Smoke streams with mask applied in steam layer set.

## Step 18

Place the light streak layer set on top of all the other layers. Within it place a layer with a small swatch of white paint applied using the Paintbrush and position it over the model's face (see Figure 8.20).

## Step 19

Change the blend mode to Overlay and apply a mask to restrict its effects to the edge of the model's face and leaf hair. This will represent the highlights reflected from above the model (see Figure 8.21).

## Step 20

Finally, give the image a little more contrast using the Curve adjustment layer (Figure 8.22).

**FIGURE 8.20**    White paint applied over the model's face.

**FIGURE 8.21**    Overlay blend mode set to white paint.

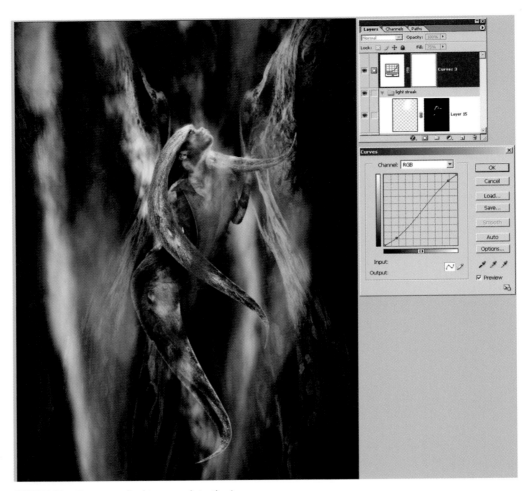

**FIGURE 8.22**    Curve applied to complete the image.

## DRAGON FLY GODDESS

This is an exercise on constructing an interior with the assistance of a few textures. To the rear of the interior will be a door that opens into another world. From this world a goddess composed of dragon fly–like wings enters into the doorway lifted up on a bed of clouds.

Let's start by creating seamless textures for the floor of the interior.

### Step 1

Access the Tutorials/ch 8 dragon fly goddess folder on the CD-ROM and open the floor texture 1.tif file (see Figure 8.23).

### Step 2

Duplicate this layer (Ctrl-J) and invert it horizontally (Edit > Transform > Flip Horizontally). Change the blend mode to lighten. Remember, that the Lighten blend mode makes all of the lower tones transparent, so by inversing the layer the dark edge is cancelled in favor of the brighter information. As a result, you will get an evenly lit texture, which is important in terms of controlling the overall tonal composition of the piece (see Figure 8.24).

**FIGURE 8.23**   Open floor texture 1.tif.

**FIGURE 8.24**   Inverse texture.

## Step 3

ON THE CD

Access the Tutorials/ch 8 dragon fly goddess folder on the CD-ROM, open the floor texture 2.tif, and place it on top to the floor texture 1 file. Change its blend mode to Soft Light (see Figures 8.25 and 8.26).

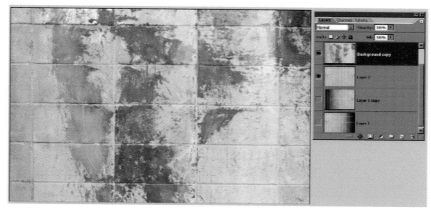

**FIGURE 8.25**    Open floor texture 2.tif.

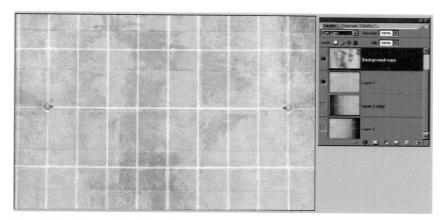

**FIGURE 8.26**    Change blend mode to Soft Light.

When finished, flatten the file so that you are working on one image.

## Step 4

Place four guides along the grout, as shown in Figure 8.27 and use Distort (Edit > Transform > Distort) to align the grout with the guides.

## Step 5

Now we will make this texture seamless. The goal is to obtain the brick pattern without the metal anchors embedded into it. We will use the Patch tool to edit it out. Activate the Patch tool and select the Source radial button on the option bar (see Figure 8.28).

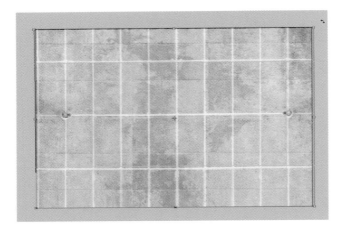

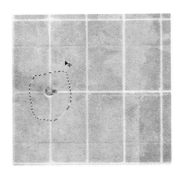

**FIGURE 8.28** Select the Patch tool.

**FIGURE 8.27** Align the grout with the guides.

Next, click and drag the selection to an area that you want to use to replace the blemish. You will see a visual update indicating how the texture is being applied (see Figure 8.29).

Apply this technique to any areas that you would like to edit. Figure 8.30 is an example of the finished piece.

## Step 6

Let's make this seamless. Start by opening the Image Size panel (Image > Image Size). Divide the pixel dimensions by two and record the results, as shown in Figure 8.31. In this example it is 1536 × 1024.

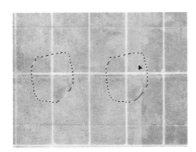

**FIGURE 8.29** Apply the Patch tool.

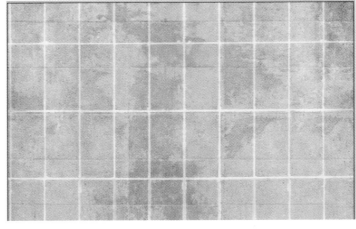

**FIGURE 8.30** Results of the Patch tool.

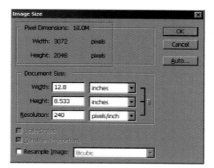

**FIGURE 8.31**    Record image size results.

Access the Offset tool (Filter > Other > Offset) and plug in the results from the previous step. Currently the image is not seamless because we can see hard edge inconsistencies in the image. Use the Patch tool to patch up the harsh edges. When complete your image will be seamless (see Figures 8.32 and 8.33).

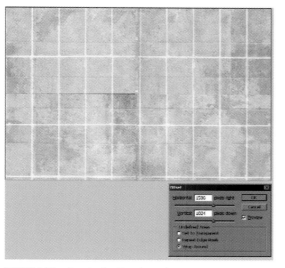

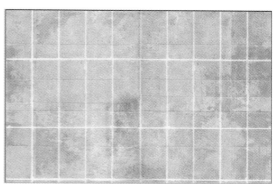

**FIGURE 8.33**    Results of Patch tool editing.

**FIGURE 8.32**    Apply the Patch tool.

## Step 7

Create a new 10 × 12-inch file at 300 ppi. Place the texture into the new image and duplicate it. Place the duplicate copy end-to-end with the original to get one long texture. Merge them into a new layer (Ctrl-alt-shift-N-E) and use the Perspective tool to obtain something like that shown in Figure 8.34.

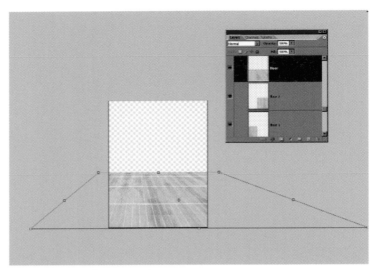

**FIGURE 8.34**   Apply perspective.

## Step 8

ON THE CD

Now that the floor has been established it needs a wall in the background. Access the Tutorials/ch 8 dragon fly goddess folder on the CD-ROM and open the metal wall.tif file (see Figure 8.35).

This texture is already seamless so place it underneath the floor and duplicate it across the entire image (see Figure 8.36).

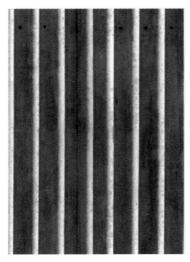

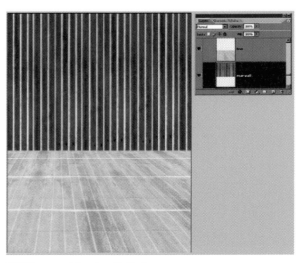

**FIGURE 8.35**   Metal wall.tif.

**FIGURE 8.36**   Metal wall tiled.

## Step 9

Place the `metal wall & door.tif` file from `Tutorials/ch 8 dragon fly goddess` on top of both layers (see Figures 8.37 and 8.38).

**FIGURE 8.37**    Metal door & wall.tif.

**FIGURE 8.38**    Place metal wall and door.

## Step 10

Duplicate the metal wall and apply a side wall on the left using the Transform and Perspective Tools. In addition add layer masks to sculpt out a space for the ceiling. Finally, apply Levels adjustment layers to add contrast to the scene (see Figure 8.39).

## Step 11

Next, enlarge the door to match the height of the ceiling and add a mask to it to match the curve of the ceiling space and to cut out the door space.

Duplicate the floor and place it in the ceiling space. Add some contrast to differentiate it from the rest of the image. Place all of the layers associated with creating the interior into a layer set called "interior" (see Figure 8.40).

**FIGURE 8.39** Add wall and layer masks as well as contrast.

**FIGURE 8.40** Add the ceiling.

## Step 12

Use the Polygonal Lasso tool to select the door in the original metal wall door file and drag and resize it to the opening of the doorway. Place it in a new Layer set above the interior layer set and title it "door" (see Figure 8.41).

**FIGURE 8.41**    Add and resize the door.

## Step 13

Use Free Transform and Perspective commands to open the door toward the viewer (see Figure 8.42).

**FIGURE 8.42**    Open the door outward.

### Step 14

We will now give the door some thickness. Use the Rectangular Marquee tool and copy and paste a long vertical sample of the door into a new layer, as shown in Figure 8.43. Darken it a bit with Levels so that the edge shows differentiation and depth.

### Step 15

Place and transform the shape to the edge of the door (see Figure 8.44).

**FIGURE 8.43**   Copy and paste selection.

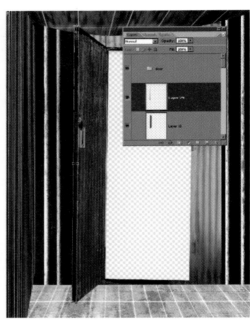

**FIGURE 8.44**   Transform the shape.

### Step 16

As shown in Figures 8.45 and 8.46, add a little more detail to the door and access the Texturizer command (Filter > Filter Gallery).

### Step 17

Since Texturizer works so well for the door edge, we will apply it to the walls and doorway as well (see Figure 8.47).

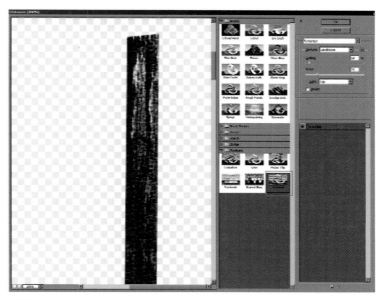

**FIGURE 8.45**    Apply texture to door edge.

**FIGURE 8.46**    Detail view of door edge.

**FIGURE 8.47**    Apply texture to the doorway and walls.

## Step 18

The light source will be coming mostly through the door, so we will create a shadow behind the door (see Figures 8.48 and 8.49).

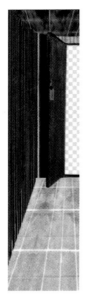

**FIGURE 8.48** Detail of the door without a shadow.

**FIGURE 8.49** Detail of the door with a shadow.

## Step 19

Make sure that you are in the floor layer and activate the Vanishing Point tool (Filter > Vanishing Point). Vanishing Point is a very cool new tool in CS2. In essence, to fool the eye into thinking that a 2D scene has three dimensions you would have to apply the use of vanishing points. Anything in the foreground will appear larger and anything in the background will look smaller. In this case if you take the ruler and follow the lines of the floor to the background you will notice that the points will intersect. The place where they intersect is the vanishing point. This creates perspective. The Vanishing Point tool allows you to edit your image while maintaining the perspective of your scene. In other words, if you select a portion of texture and drag it throughout the scene it will enlarge or reduce according to your perspective. This is a very handy tool indeed. Let's play with it.

You need to start by defining your perspective. This is done with the Create Plane Tool. Select it and apply a grid that matches the outlines of the floor tiles as shown in Figure 8.50. Notice that the grid has what appears to be handlebars on the corners and sides that are very similar to the Free Transform tool. This is because you can re-size it to include the areas that you want to edit. You can also extend other perspective grids off of the original by Ctrl-clicking and dragging the center control handles on each side to establish vertical perspective as well. For this example let's concentrate on the floor area and establish its perspective. You don't need to worry about any other portions of the scene, so click on the two sides as well as the top and delete them by hitting the delete key on the keyboard. Let's work with the floor grid only.

**FIGURE 8.50**    Create a grid.

## Step 20

Click and hold on the handles of the floor perspective grid and extend them beyond the areas that you want to work with—in this case, it's the floor (see Figure 8.51).

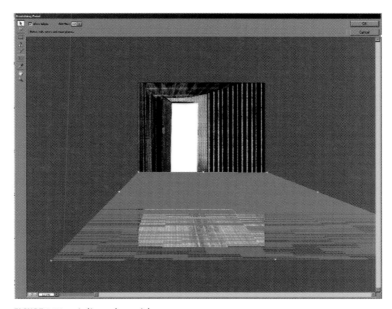

**FIGURE 8.51**    Adjust the grid.

## Step 21

Set the options according to Figure 8.52. We will use the healing technique to add more uniformity to the floor.

**FIGURE 8.52**   Adjust the options.

## Step 22

With the Selection tool activated in the options, select the area that you would like to take the texture from. Hold the Ctrl-shift while dragging to duplicate the selected texture over any location of your image. The magic is that the perspective that you applied is also applied to the chosen shape you are dragging (see Figure 8.53).

The same can be done using the Stamp tool option. Hold the Alt key and sample a texture that you like. As you place the mouse around the floor area, notice how it becomes larger or smaller relative to the perspective. Use this in addition to the selection technique to even out the texture patterns so that they are not so predictable in relation to the original file (see Figure 8.54).

## Step 23

ON THE CD

Place the ocean view.tif from Tutorials/ch 8 dragon fly goddess underneath the interior wall and transform it to your liking. Apply a Levels adjustment layer and darken the entire image. This will serve to set the background apart from the lighting (see Figure 8.55).

**FIGURE 8.53**    Selection in Vanishing Point.

**FIGURE 8.54**    Stamp tool in Vanishing Point.

**FIGURE 8.55**    Apply a Levels adjustment layer.

## Step 24

Finally, create a new layer set above the door titled "doorway light flares." Create a series of light sources coming from the doorway. Use the Rectangular Marquee tool and fill it with white. Change the blend mode to Overlay and add a little Gaussian Blur to the shape. Use Free Transform (Ctrl-T) and Perspective to alter the shapes as shown in Figure 8.56.

**FIGURE 8.56**   Create light falloff.

## PLACING THE GODDESS

The goddess will enter the room through the door on a bed of clouds. We will also give her a set of wings.

### Step 1

ON THE CD

Place the beach portrait.tif from the Tutorials/ch 8 dragon fly goddess folder into a layer set. Call the layer set "model." Use the Transform and Perspective tools to mold the image to look as if the model is coming out into the interior space, as shown in Figure 8.57.

### Step 2

Apply a layer mask to isolate the background (see Figures 8.58 and 8.59).

**FIGURE 8.57**    Place the model into the scene.

**FIGURE 8.58**    Results of layer mask.

**FIGURE 8.59**    View of layer mask.

### Step 3

Duplicate the model and change the blend mode to Screen to brighten her up a bit (see Figure 8.60).

**FIGURE 8.60**    Duplicate layer.

### Step 4

Add some Motion Blur (Filter > Blur > Motion Blur) to give the model a sense of flying toward the viewer. Use a layer mask to limit the blur (see Figure 8.61).

### Step 5

Add a shadow on a separate layer and place it underneath the model. Use the technique you learned from Chapter 3 to create the shadow. When finished, add a burning and dodging layer by filling a new layer with 50% gray and changing the blend mode to Overlay. Use your burning and dodging tools on this layer to darken the back half of the model (see Figure 8.62). This is a non-destructive way to darken and brighten your image.

**FIGURE 8.61**    Add Motion Blur.

**FIGURE 8.62**    Add shadow and shading.

## CREATING WINGS FOR THE GODDESS

We will take a template of a dragon fly wing to create a single wing. We will duplicate the wing to be placed into the model, and then we will add effects to make it look like she is flapping her wings.

### Step 1

ON THE CD

Access the Tutorials/ch 8 dragon fly goddess folder on the CD-ROM and open the wings template.jpg file. You will see the outline of a wing on its own layer (see Figure 8.63). (If you prefer to jump to Step 1 of Adding Wings to the Goddess, you can use the dragon fly wing merged.tif from the Tutorial/ch 8 dragon fly goddess folder).

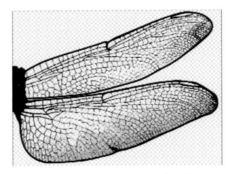

**FIGURE 8.63**    Open wings template.jpg.

### Step 2

Now let's add a little more detail to the wing. We will add smaller vein details throughout the wings by using filter effects.

Create a new layer and fill it with 50% gray. Then access the Stained Glass filter through the Filter Gallery (Filter > Filter Gallery), as shown in Figure 8.64.

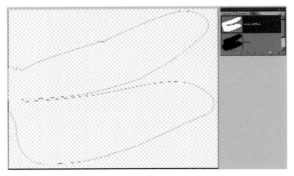

**FIGURE 8.64**    Stained Glass filter.

## Step 3

When complete, apply Threshold (Image > Adjust > Threshold) and alter the tones to black and white only. Threshold's purpose is to take any color image and alter it to a 2-bit result. In other words, you will get only black or white by expanding black when the slider is moved to the right or contracting it so that white dominates when you move the slider to the left.

In this case, the wing veins are white. We want them to be the opposite tone, so hit Ctrl-I (Inverse) to inverse the tones (see Figure 8.65).

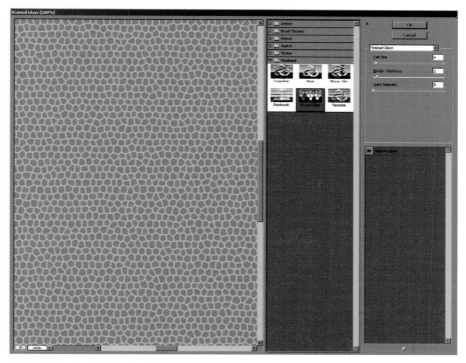

**FIGURE 8.65**    Apply Threshold.

## Step 4

Use the Pen tool to create an outline of the wing and make a vector mask using the newly filled texture. Change its blend mode to Overlay so that you will be able to see through it to the next pattern you are about to create (see Figures 8.66 and 8.67).

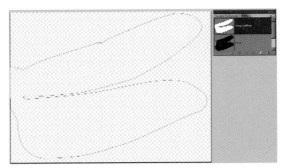

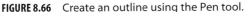

FIGURE 8.66   Create an outline using the Pen tool.

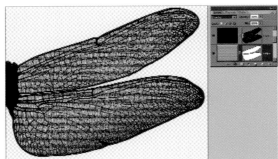

FIGURE 8.67   Create a vector mask.

### Step 5

Turn off all of the layers to help you see the results of this step. Select two shades of green for your background and foreground layers. Create a new layer below the vein detail and fill it with greenish clouds (Filter > Render > Clouds) and change the blend mode to Overlay. Use the outline of the wing to create a vector mask as you did in Step 7, but this time use the texture pattern that you have just created (see Figure 8.68).

### Step 6

Use the same vector outline to mask out an additional layer filled with a cloud pattern. In this example a yellow hue is used for the cloud patterns. When complete, change the opacity to around 45% so the entire image has some transparency. Merge the layers (Ctrl-alt-shift-N-E), as shown in Figure 8.70. Let's place the wings to create the goddess.

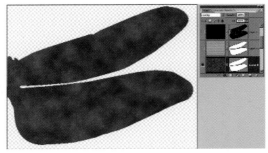

FIGURE 8.68   Create a vector mask using the texture pattern that you created.

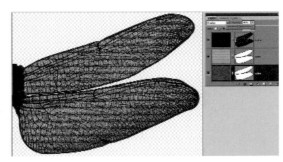

FIGURE 8.69   The results of a layer filled with green clouds.

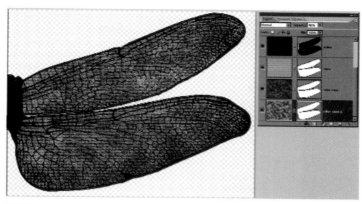

**FIGURE 8.70**    Merge the layers.

## ADDING WINGS TO THE GODDESS

### Step 1

Place your wing into the goddess image underneath the model layer set. Duplicate and transform it as shown in Figure 8.71.

**FIGURE 8.71**    Place the wing into the goddess image.

## Step 2

Duplicate the transformed wing and offset it using the Transform tool. Add some Motion Blur to give it the illusion of motion (see Figure 8.72).

**FIGURE 8.72**    Duplicate the transformed wing.

Repeat this process several times to produce something similar to that shown in Figure 8.73. Next, place them into a layer set titled "left wing."

## Step 3

Duplicate the layer set titled left wing and rename it "right wing." Although this example is titled left wing copy it is a good idea to keep better organized. Transform the entire layer set contents to match Figure 8.74.

Make sure all of the contents in the folder are visible or you will not be able to transform the layer set. Therefore, have only the elements that you want to be part of your file in it and delete any unwanted layers.

**FIGURE 8.73**    Repeat the duplication process.

**FIGURE 8.74**    Transform the layer set.

## Step 4

Above the model layer set create a new layer and fill it with white. Reduce its opacity to around 50% (see Figure 8.75).

**FIGURE 8.75** Fill layer with white.

Next, apply a mask filled with black and paint in light streaks coming forward to the viewer. Apply them in the gaps of the arms, legs, and wings (see Figure 8.76).

**FIGURE 8.76** Add light streaks.

## Step 5

Duplicate the light streak layer and continue to add to the effect using different types of brushes. You have experience with creating your own brushes to play with a variety of strokes and shapes. When you are done, place all of your layers in a layer set titled "light streaks." Figures 8.77 and 8.78 show this progression.

**FIGURE 8.77**    Add light streaks.

**FIGURE 8.78**    Add more light streaks.

## ADDING A FEW DETAILS

We will add just a few small details to make our composition more interesting.

### Step 1

Create a new layer below the right wing layer set and fill it with white. This will give some haze effect to the rear of the goddess. Reduce its opacity (see Figure 8.79).

**FIGURE 8.79**    Add rear haze.

### Step 2

Access the floor layer and add a Curves adjustment layer to darken the floor. Use a gradient on its mask to restrict the effects more toward the rear of the floor, as shown in Figure 8.80.

### Step 3

Use Liquefy (Filter > Liquefy) to misshape the ear, which will help to give the goddess an other-worldly appearance (see Figure 8.81).

**FIGURE 8.80**    Add a Curves adjustment layer to darken the floor.

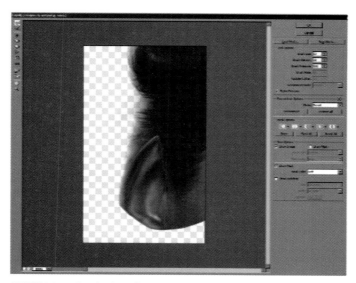

**FIGURE 8.81**    Apply Liquefy.

## Step 4

Add the light source by using the standard Lens Flare technique. Add a Levels adjustment layer to make slight contrast increases (see Figure 8.82).

**FIGURE 8.82**    Add light source and contrast adjustments.

## Step 5

Every goddess has to come with clouds. So let's create some.

This is really not a complicated process. We will use the same techniques of transforming and masking to place and resize the cloud image.

Go to the Tutorials/ch 8 dragon fly goddess folder and open the cloud.tif. Start by creating the "cloud foreground" layer set and place the cloud.tif in it. Desaturate the cloud image so that you are left only with white and gray tones. Change its blend mode to Overlay so that the gray patterns become transparent leaving you with only the white puffy clouds. Duplicate the layer several times and resize each layer to overlap with one another. Use layer masking to blend the clouds with one another (see Figures 8.83 and 8.84).

**FIGURE 8.83**    Cloud.tif.

**FIGURE 8.84**    Create the clouds using Free Transform and Masking.

## ADDING FINAL EFFECTS

The nik Color Efex Pro 2.0 filter is wonderful to use to give the image a polished look in the finishing stages. This does not mean that you should concentrate on using it for this purpose only. Experiment with using the filters during intermediate steps as well. Try changing the results blend mode like we did in the Chapter 4 meteor tutorial. Always experiment.

### Step 1

Apply the Graduated Neutral Density filter, as shown in Figure 8.85 to increase the density of the floor with little or no effect to the upper portion of the composition. Follow the settings shown in Figure 8.86. The final results are shown in Figure 8.87.

### Step 2

Apply the Bicolor Moss filter on top of the Graduated Neutral Density results to give the image a different atmosphere (see Figures 8.88 through 8.90).

**FIGURE 8.85**    Apply Graduated Neutral Density filter.

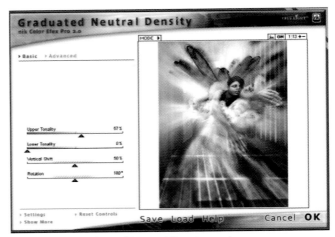

**FIGURE 8.86**    Graduated Neutral Density settings.

**FIGURE 8.87**    Results of Graduated Neutral Density filter.

**FIGURE 8.88** Apply Bicolor Moss filter.

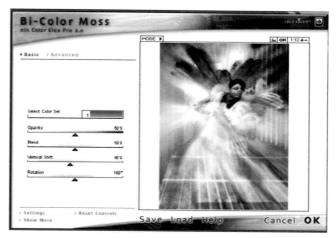

**FIGURE 8.89** Bicolor Moss settings.

**FIGURE 8.90** Results of Bicolor Moss filter.

## Step 3

Apply the Graduated Neutral Density filter again on top of the Bicolor Moss to increase the density of the floor with little or no effect to the upper portion of the composition (see Figure 8.91).

Finally, edit the masks to allow the clouds to take on the original color, as shown in Figure 8.92.

The final results are shown in Figure 8.93.

**FIGURE 8.91**    Reapply Graduated Neutral Density filter.

**FIGURE 8.92**    Edit the Bicolor Moss masks.

**FIGURE 8.93**    Final results.

## WHAT YOU HAVE LEARNED

- How to make seamless textures
- How to apply Vanishing Point
- How to create paths from selections
- How to custom create fog light rays
- Creative applications of Color Efex Pro 2.0

# ABOUT THE CD-ROM

The CD-ROM included with *Advanced Photoshop CS2 Trickery & FX* includes all files necessary to complete the tutorials in the book. It also includes the images from the book in full color, and demos for you to use while working through the tutorials and exercises.

## CD FOLDERS

**Images:** All of the images from within the book are in full color in Jpeg format. These files are set up by chapter.

**Tutorials:** All of the files necessary to complete the tutorials in the book including, backgrounds, textures, and images. These files are all in Tif formats, which can be read by most graphic applications. They are set up in folders designated by chapter and tutorial heading under the Tutorial folder.

**Demos:** We have included a demo of Photoshop CS2 (PC only), nik multimedia's nik Color Efex Pro 2.0 and nik Sharpener Pro 2.0.

The first is a demo version of Photoshop CS2 for Windows. This is a 30-day time-limited fully working demo. Contact *www.adobe.com* to get student or full prices if you are interested in downloading the Macintosh version, or in purchasing this powerful package.

The second application is a demo version of nik multimedia's Color Efex Pro 2.0 (Windows). This is a fully functioning package with no time limitations however a nik watermark stamp will appear on rendered images. A PDF user's manual is included in the nik Color Efex Pro folder. See *www.nikmultimedia.com* for more information.

The third application is a demo version of nik multimedia's nik Sharpener Pro 2.0 (Windows). This is a fully functioning package with no time limitations, however a watermark stamp will appear on rendered images. A PDF user's manual is included in the nik Sharpener Pro folder. See *www.nikmultimedia.com* for more information.

## MINIMUM SYSTEM REQUIREMENTS

For both systems you will need Photoshop CS2. The trial version for the PC is included on this CD-ROM and will let you work through the projects with no limitations except that it is time limited to 30 days. The Macintosh version is available for download at www.adobe.com.

### Windows

- Intel Pentium III or 4 processor
- Microsoft Windows 2000 with Service Pack 4, or Windows XP with Service Pack 1 or 2
- 384 MB of RAM to run any one creative application with Adobe Bridge and Version Cue Workspace
- Additional RAM required to run multiple applications simultaneously (512 MB to 1 GB recommended)
- 2 GB of available hard-disk space to install all applications (installation of common files requires at least 1 GB on primary hard disk)
- 1,024 × 768 monitor resolution with 16-bit video card (24-bit screen display recommended)
- CD-ROM drive
- For Adobe PostScript printers: PostScript Level 2 or PostScript 3
- Internet or phone connection required for product activation
- QuickTime 6.5 required for multimedia features

Broadband Internet connection required for Adobe Stock Photos and additional services. (The Adobe Stock Photos service may not be available in all countries, languages, and currencies and is subject to change. Use of the service is governed by the Adobe Stock Photos Terms of Service. For details, please visit Adobe Stock Photos.)

### Macintosh

- PowerPC G4 or G5 processor
- Mac OS X v.10.2.8 through v.10.4 (10.3.4 through 10.4 recommended; G5 requires v.10.3 or later), Java Runtime Environment 1.4.1
- 384 MB of RAM to run any one creative application with Adobe Bridge and Version Cue Workspace
- Additional RAM required to run multiple applications simultaneously (512 MB to 1 GB recommended)
- 3 GB of available hard-disk space to install all applications (installation of common files requires at least 1 GB on primary hard disk)

- 1,024 × 768 monitor resolution with 16-bit video card (24-bit screen display recommended)
- CD-ROM drive
- For Adobe PostScript printers: PostScript Level 2 or PostScript 3
- Internet or phone connection required for product activation
- QuickTime 6.5 required for multimedia features

Broadband Internet connection required for Adobe Stock Photos and additional services (The Adobe Stock Photos service may not be available in all countries, languages, and currencies and is subject to change. Use of the service is governed by the Adobe Stock Photos Terms of Service. For details, please visit Adobe Stock Photos.)

## NIK COLOR EFEX PRO 2.0 AND NIK SHARPENER PRO 2.0 (WINDOWS) SYSTEM REDQUIREMENTS

For both systems you will need nik Color Efex Pro 2.0. The trial versions for the PC are included on this CD-ROM and will let you work through the projects, with no limitations except that a watermark will be placed on the final results.

For Macintosh versions of the demos, please visit *www.nikmultimedia. com*.

### Windows

- Windows 98 Second Edition (SE) through Windows XP, or later.
- 300 MHz Pentium or better (800 MHz or faster recommended).
- 128 MB RAM (256 MB recommended).
- 800 × 600 screen resolution at 16-bit color depth  (1024 × 768 at 24-bit depth recommended).
- 300 MB of hard-disk space for the Complete Edition, 190 MB of hard disk space for the Select Edition, and 90 MB of hard-disk space for the Standard Edition required.
- Image editing application that accepts Photoshop Plug-Ins.

### Macintosh

- Mac OS 9.2.x and OS 10.1.5 or later.
- G3 processor or better (G4 or better recommended).
- 128 MB RAM (256 MB recommended).
- 800 × 600 screen resolution at 16-bit color depth (1024 × 768 at 24-bit depth recommended).

- 480 MB of hard disk space for the Complete Edition, 290 MB of hard disk space for the Select Edition, and 130 MB of hard disk space for the Standard Edition required.
- Image editing application that accepts Photoshop Plug-Ins.

### nik Color Efex Pro 2.0 Selective Tool

**Windows Operating System:**
Windows 98 through XP.
Adobe Photoshop 5.5 through CS or Adobe Photoshop Elements 1 & 2.0.

**Macintosh Operating System:**
Mac OS 10.1.5 or later.
Adobe Photoshop 7 through CS & Adobe Photoshop Elements 2.0.

**Note for nik Sharpener:**
nik Sharpener filters are Adobe Photoshop compatible Plug-Ins that are compatible with the following operating systems:
Windows 98SE/ME/NT/2000/XP
Macintosh OS 10.2.4 through 10.4.x

nik Sharpener is compatible with the following image editing applications:

- Adobe Photoshop 5.5 through CS2
- Adobe Photoshop Elements 1 through 3.0
- Adobe PhotoDeluxe
- Adobe Photoshop LE
- Corel Paint Shop Pro
- Corel PHOTOPAINT
- Microsoft Digital Image Pro
- Ulead PhotoImpact

## INSTALLATION

To use this CD-ROM, you just need to make sure that your system matches at least the minimum system requirements. Each demo has its own installation instructions and you should contact the developer directly if you have any problems installing the demo. The images and tutorial files are in the Tif file format and should be usable with any graphics application.

# INDEX